Volume 2

I0101100

SATANISM: AN OLD WORLD ORDER

THE LIFE OF " ☯ M "

In the beginning of "Time", there was "**OM**"... *The Supreme Master of Creativity*. For "**OM**" created He, "Him", fr**om** the construct...of His **OW**n design. The Master's voice, was a t**wo**-edge s**wo**rd...that contained the creative **wo**rds of Life.

For He... taught..."Him", that all **wo**rds were simply the Genesis of its **ow**n ends. {**S**word & word**S**}. Within the creative **wo**rds of Master "**OM**", a list of secret numbers were concealed fr**om** Mankind; for t**wo** thousand years. N**ow**, as the clocks of do**om** did sound their toll of Death, the **MO**nad of Master "**OM**" did arise... fr **OM** ... f **O**rm.

With one swift horizontal **MO**vement of His **wo**rdiacious s**wo**rd, Master "**OM**" created a scythe-of-light that slashed across the night-of-void. In a flash of pure brilliance, The Master "**OM**" revealed the light-of-truth. Within the frame **wo**rk of pure-light, the truth-of-time was sh**ow**n...to all, **w**h**o** had gone in search of...Truth and... for Master "**OM**"!

In the brilliance of pure light, Time, was sh**ow**n to be in relation to its **ow**n Destiny. The long hours of enduring the dark-side of truth had reached its final end. Behind the shad**ow** of time, stood Master "**OM**", the **OM**en of **OM**ega.

With a Vertical-bl**ow** across the horizontal plane of existence, the s**wo**rd of Master "**OM**" did indeed, ref**orm**' the path... to the Righteous-Cross. ["N.E.W.S"].

North
tseW A☯Ω East
htuoS

It was indeed, this **MO**tion of Master "**OM**" that lent Time its <Wings-of-Flight>. Once again, the Mystical **Sw**ord of **wo**rd**S** did Twitch within The **W**h**o**le frame-**wo**rk of Master "**OM**"...and once again...Time was divided into its har**mo**nious rhythm of order.

Each **MO**nad of Life had its **ow**n Time Scale of Identity and Rhythm. Each Hour of Fate had it's **ow**n plane of existence...and every minute was but a second...within this Time Frame of One's Mystical Number. On this Time-Plane of Consciousness, No Life Could C**om**prehend its **ow**n existence without the due consideration of it's Opposite Numbers. Thus, The Mystical Numbers in the Creative "**wo**"rds of Master "**OM**" existed with the Kn**ow**ledge of Identifying it's "**ow**"n Genesis...with it's **ow**n **OM**ega.

by **THE GRAND MASTER**

To be continued...

THE SCIENCE OF NUMBERS:

In the Kingdom of Numbers, the "Life Aspect" of 'zero' (0) is *Primal...*In Number.

It is the foundation and head of all calculations. Without "0", there would have been no Genesis to Life. In the beginning...there was 'nothing' ("0"), and from 'nothing'... there came 'something', and from that 'something', came 'Something-else'. Whatever came first, second or third...out of 'nothing', does not really matter. What does matter is the undenying fact... that when "They" did come, "They" came in a Numerical order from the first "0" to the last "9", and anything else beyond that, was 'nothing' more than a repetition of the same order. Hence, History...repeats itself, in a Numerical order.

THE LIFE OF ☯M

In the beginning of "Time", there was "**OM**"...*The Supreme Master of Creativity*.
For "**OM**" created "He...Him", from the construct... of His **ow**n design. The Master's voice, was a **two**-edge s**wo**rd...that contained the creative **wo**rds of Life. For "He"... taught..."Him", that all **wo**rds were simply the Genesis of its **ow**n ends.{**S**word & word**S**}. Within the creative **wo**rds of Master "**OM**", a list of secret numbers were concealed fr**om** Mankind; for **two** thousand years. N**ow**, as the clocks of do**om** did sound their toll of Death, the **MO**nad of Master "**OM**" did arise...fr**OM** ...f **Orm.** With one swift horizontal **MO**vement of His **wo**rdiacious s**wo**rd, Master "**OM**" created a scythe-of-light to slash across the night-of-void. In a flash of pure brilliance, The Master "**OM**" revealed the light-of-truth. Within the frame-**wo**rk of pure-light, the truth-of-time was sh**ow**n...to all, **wh**o had gone in search of... Master "**OM**".

In light, time, was sh**ow**n to be in relation to its **ow**n Destiny. The long hours of enduring the dark-side of truth had reached its final end. Behind the shad**ow** of time, stood Master "**OM**", the **OM**en of **OM**ega.

With a Vertical-bl**ow** across the horizontal plane of existance, the s**wo**rd of Master "**OM**" did indeed, ref**orm**' the path...to the Righteous-Cross.["N.E.W.S"]

North
tseW A☯Ω East
htuoS

It was indeed, this **MO**tion of Master "**OM**" that lent Time its <Wings-of-Flight>. Once again, the Mystical **Sw**ord of word**S** did Twitch within The **W**hole frame-**wo**rk of Master "**OM**"...and once again...Time was divided into its har**mo**nious rhythm of order.

Each **MO**nad of Life had its **ow**n Time Scale of Identity and Rhythm. Each Hour of Fate had it's **ow**n plane of existance...and every minute was but a second...within this Time Frame of One's Mystical Number. On this Time-Plane of Consciousness, No Life Could **Com**prehend its **ow**n existence without the due consideration of it's Opposite Numbers.Thus, The Mystical Numbers in the Creative "**wo**"rds of Master "**OM**" existed with the Kn**ow**ledge of Identifying it's "**ow**"n Genesis...with it's **own OM**ega.

```
                              N
                              o
                              r
                              t
                             *H

                    W ) est    eas ( T

                             H*
                              t
                              u
                              o
                              S
```

NOTAS:

    W -->   est   _eas <-- T

        *69...= Winds...*Of Change

SATANISM & VOODOO

TRACING THE "I.D." OF 'THE BEAST OF REVELATION[*666/616].

We are now dealing with the **TREE-of-LIFE** (**Cabala Master*):

"O"

👆

THE DIETY

```
                    ⓪  ⓪  H
        U           ①
        N           ②
            ❸  ③   ③  O
        H           ④
        O   ❾  ⑤
                    ⑥  ⑥  L
        L           ⑦
        Y   ❻  ⑧
                    ⑨  ⑨  Y
                _____
            *45    GODS...'Zen'
```

NOTAS:

DIVISION of the TRINITY: The Symbol of *3, 6 + 9 is the Occult Symbol representing the Holy TRINITY of: Father, Son and Holy "Ghost". They are Holy on account of Their ability to remain in Their NUMERICAL order of Birth. However, the same cannot be said about the Symbol of *3, 9 + 6., as They represent all the Fallen Sons of GoD. They fell by the Wisdom of Their own stupidity, for They tried to play GOD...over 'all' of Man-kind. Their Divinity can be attested to by "The Genetic-of-Blood"... which was simply Mathematical and Divine.

Test:

TRINITY

Un-Holy		HOLY		
3	+	3	= 6	
9	+	6	= 15 and 1+ 5 = 6	
6	+	9	= 15 and 1+ 5 = 6	

1 + 2 .... = 3
4 + 5 .... = 9   TRINITY = *115 X 9 =*1035   1035
7 + 8 =15 and 1 + 5 = 6

minus   369   or   - 666
------   -------
666   369

T	=	20
R	=	18
I	=	9
N	=	14
I	=	9
T	=	20
Y	=	25

115
x 9   (No:"9" represents SIN.)

N.B. *369 + 666 =   1035

THE POPE'S MOTTO {*Symbol of the Beast...*Pyramid of the Dead}

VICARIUS =	102	The	= 33	The	=	33
FiLii =	45	Three	= 56	Triple	=	80
Dei =	18	Sixes	= 76	Six	=	52
	*165		165			165

NOTAS: The Melodic Minor Scale of Names, Places and People.

GROUP "A". Side-by-Side:

1) Charlie (*56) Chaplan (*55)
2) Michael (*51) *and* Janet (*50)
3) Cinema (*45) Talk (*44)
4) Emperor (*90) Selassie (*89)
5) Jesus (*74) *and* Joseph (*73)
6) Anton (*64) La Vey (*65)
7) Eliphas (*70) Levi Del (*69)
8) African (*52) Fiasco (*53)
9) Saint (*63) Peter (*64)

GROUP "B". Ten above...Ten below:

1) Father *58 *and* Son *48... *are One.*
2) Land *31 *and* King *41...*are One.*
3) King *41 *and* Chief *31... *are One.*
4) Home *41 *and* Land *31... *are One.*
5) Knight *69 *and* Dragon *59... *are One*
6) God Father *84 *and* God Son *74... *are One.*
7) God Father *84 and Jesus *74...*are One.*
8) Jesus *74 *and* Peter *64... *are One.*
9) Hamlet *59 *and the* Ghost *69... *are One.*

GROUP "C". Opposites:

1) Moon *57... Diameter *75
2) Human *57... Skull *75
3) Time *47... Moves *74
4) Time *47... Stuck *74
5) Today *65... Past *56
6) Two *58... Squared *85
7) Tunnel *86... Passage *68
8) Daughter *84... Son *48
9) South *83... Africa *38

GROUP "D". Identical Twins:

1) Rock *47... Monad *47
2) Rock *47... Legend *47
3) Resides *79... In Light *79
4) Round *72... World *72
5) Animals *69... Jungle *69
6) Hade's *37... Hell *37
7) Fat Lady *69... Fat Boy *69
8) Sex *48... Trade *48
9) Word *60... Order *60

GROUP "E". Identical(*Bi-Twins).

1) The God Head *77... Immanuel *88
2) Christ *77... Begotten *88
3) Electrical *88... Current *99
4) Ancient *66... Matter *77
5) Space *44... &... Sky *55
6) The *33... Brain *44
7) Judges *66... Legal Liar *77
8) Inter (*66)... Sky (*55)
9) Lunar (*66)... Matter (*77)

The Law Of Numerology

(**1st Law)

Any Number that is in 'The centre' of its relative group Number(s), is squared (**double the Value) to the power of its neighbouring Number as well as opposite to its own numerical value. In these few examples, I shall *"High-Light"* the PRIMAL-NUMBER (**Any number in the Centre) in order to calculate the Numerical Relationship shared with all Numbers from 'zero to Infinity'.

EXAMPLES:

	38			73			27			45			31	
27	**28**	29	62	**63**	64	16	**17**	18	34	**35**	36	20	**21**	22
	18													
	>82		53			7			25			11		
				>36			**>71**			**>53**			**>12**	

Number *28; *63; *17; *35; and **21* are our five Primal-Numbers.
Number *82; *36; *71; *53; and **12* are the total reversal of the above "5" Primal Numbers.

*A = No: 27 and 29 are the Left and Right of Prime No: *28... therefore,

$$2 \quad x \quad 28 \quad = \quad \mathbf{56}... \text{ and}$$

$$\text{*27} \quad + \quad \text{*29} \quad = \quad \mathbf{56}$$

No: 38 and 18 are the Head and Feet of Prime No: *28... therefore,

$$\text{*38} \quad + \quad \text{*18} \quad = \quad \mathbf{56}$$

*B= No: 62 and 64 are the Left and Right of Prime No: *63... therefore,

$$2 \quad x \quad 63 \quad = \quad \mathbf{126}... \text{ and}$$

$$\text{*62} \quad + \quad \text{*64} \quad = \quad \mathbf{126}$$

No: 73 and 53 are the Head and Feet of Prime No: *63... therefore,

$$\text{*73} \quad + \quad \text{*53} \quad = \quad \mathbf{126}$$

*C= No: 16 and 18 are the Left and Right of Prime No: *17... therefore,

$$2 \quad x \quad 17 \quad = \quad \mathbf{34}... \text{ and}$$

$$\text{*16} \quad + \quad \text{*18} \quad = \quad \mathbf{34}$$

No: 27 and *7 are the Head and Feet of Prime No: *17... therefore,

$$\text{*27} \quad + \quad \text{*7} \quad = \quad \mathbf{34}$$

*D= No: 34 and 36 are the Left and Right of Prime No: *35... therefore,

$$2 \quad x \quad 35 \quad = \quad \mathbf{70}... \text{ and}$$

$$\text{*34} \quad + \quad \text{*36} \quad = \quad \mathbf{70}$$

No: 45 and 25 are the Head and Feet of Prime No: *35... therefore,

$$\text{*45} \quad + \quad \text{*25} \quad = \quad \mathbf{70}$$

*E= No:20 and 22 are the Left and Right of Prime No: *21... therefore,

$$2 \times \quad 21 \quad = \quad \textbf{42}... \text{ and}$$

$$*20 \quad + \quad *22 \quad = \quad \textbf{42}$$

No: 31 and 11 are the Head and Feet of Prime No: *21... therefore,

$$*31 \quad + \quad *11 \quad = \quad \textbf{42}$$

***NOTAS*: MODERN ELECTRONIC{S}:**

The Same formula(e) is applicable to all electronic equipment, such as Telephones and Calculators. The basic difference is that the *Numbers-Order(*Configuration) is *REVERSED(*96).

CALCULATOR'S NUMBER ORDER: (*258)

7	8	9
4	5	6
1	2	3

TELEPHONE(s) NUMBER ORDER: (*252)

1	2	3
4	5	6
7	8	9

N.B.!

The *NUMBER in the *CENTRE of any amount of Numbers, is always the *Double-Up; of <u>all</u> the other Numbers surrounding it. This is exactly what is meant by the Equation of *ENERGY BEING EQUAL TO M/C².

*A Number (*74) is *A Magnetic (*73) *ENERGY (*74); Whilst M/C Squared denotes, inter alia:

"M" stands for MAGNETIC-GAP (*96) and "C" stands for the *Character's (*96).
These *Characters *ARE MAGNETIC (*96)...*IN SOUND (*96)...*IN VOICES (*96) and *IN NUMBER (*96).

Hence, *NUMERICAL (*96) *CALCULATOR (*106)...(*96 + *106 =*202= *The Energy of a NUMBER).

The *NUMERICAL-ORDER (*156) is *RELATIVE (*NUMBERS, *ELECTRON, *CELERITAS) to the following *CHARACTERISTICS (*156):

> *Radio Activity
> *Atomic Nucleus
> *Polarization
> *NEWS Nucleus
> *The Classic Catch-22

SQUARING-UP THE NUMBERS FORMAT:

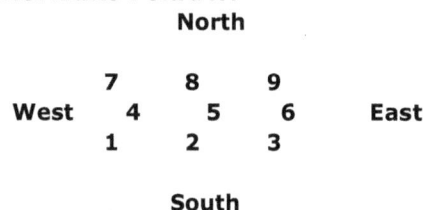

North

	7	8	9	
West	4	5	6	East
	1	2	3	

South

As No:5 is in *<u>The Centre</u> of the above <u>Numerical</u>-Order, it is Double the Value of its *Eight Surrounding Neighbours.

These '8' surrounding *NUMBERS (*92) are scientifically referred to as the *ELECTRON (*92) of an *ATOM (*49) {*EIGHT= *49}

SOLUTION:

a) 2 x 5 = 10   and   4 + 6 = 10
b) 8 + 2 = 10
c) 7 + 3 = 10
d) 9 + 1 = 10
e) 2 x 2 = 4   and   1 + 3 = 4
f) 2 x 4 = 8   and   7 + 1 = 8
g) 2 x 6 = 12   and   9 + 3 = 12
h) 2 x 8 = 16   and   7 + 9 = 16

The "1st Law" of Numerology is applicable to:

a) Names of People and Places.

b) All Word(s) and Sentences.

c) All Publications that expresses itself in terms of *The Roman Alphabet (*159). This includes all Religious Publications, from Christianity, Judaism, Islam, Hinduism, Buddhism, Dow-ism.

d) Newspapers, Magazines, Leaflets, Adverts, Periodicals, Comics, Science Publications and so on.

THE MAGNETIC CHARACTERISTICS OF WORDS AND NAMES:

A "Word, Name or Sentence" are all Relative to Magnetism. They all have the ability to jump around one another, *In union (*96) of a *Magnetic-*Dance (*72 + 27 = *Current/*Thought).

EXAMPLES:

a) "IT's (*48) NOT (*49)-
..............................*NOT OVER (*109) *UNTIL THE (*109)-
....*FAT LADY (*69) *SINGS (*68)".

b) *GOOD MORNING (*131)
....*SOUTH AFRICA (*121).

c) *YESTERDAY (*122)
...............................*TODAY AND TOMORROW (*221).

d) *ROSE AND CROSS (*150)
....*ROSICRUCIANS (*149)

e) *PEARL OF (*73)
.........................*WISDOM (*83).

f) *PAY (*42) ....*FOR THE (*72)...*RIGHT (*62)
..............*GET (*32)
...............................*THE (*33)
....*LEFT (*43)
....*FREE (*34).

g) *PUSS (*75)
...................*IN BOOT (*75).

h) *ORLANDO (*79)
............................*PIRATE (*69)
....*ONE (*34)
....*NIL (*35)
....*ONE (*34)
....*GOAL (*35).

i) *ONE UNDER (*96)
..............................*CONTROL (*97).

j) *THE (*33)
.................*ONE (*34)
................................*CHANCE (*34)
....*TO (*35)
....*COME (*36)
....*CLEAN (*35).

k) *NEPTUNE (*95)
..........................*TRITON (*96)
....*POSEIDON (*97)
....*GOD HIMSELF (*98)
....*JUDGEMENT (*99)

l) *STAR (*58)
...................*SIGNS (*68)
...............................by..*WILLIAM (*79)
....*SMITH (*69).

m) *NULL (*59)
.................*AND VOID (*69)

n) *LATE (*38)
...................*NITE (*48)
.....................................*GRILL (*58).

o) *LOOK (*53)
...................*LEFT (*43)
....................................*NOW (*52)
....*RIGHT (*62)
....*THEN (*47)
....*CROSS (*74).

p) *CONCAVE (*63)
............................*NORMAL (*73)
....*CONVEX (*83).

q) *BITTER (*74)
.......................*SOUR (*73)
....*SWEET (*72)
....*SPICES (*71).

In the above '17' examples, You will notice how a *WORDED *MESSAGE can, inter alia,

1) *JUMP (*60) *WORD (*60).
2) *JUMPS (*79) *WORDS (*79) or *STORY (*97).
3) *UNITE (*69) *TEXT (*69).
4) *UNTIE (*69) *TEXT (*69).
5) *JUMPS BACK (*96) *INTO BALANCE (*96) *AFTER BODY (*96) *OF ITS (*69) *MESSAGE (*69)
*RE-GOES (*69) *PRINTS (*96) *PUBLISHED (*96) *By RED-TAPE (*96) *FROM SPACE (*96),
*TO YOU (*96) *THE PUBLIC (*96).

The *TWENTY-SIX (*159) Letters of *THE ROMAN ALPHABET (*159) are *Magnetic by Nature (*178).
They represent the *CORPUS CHRISTI/*THE CREATION WORD which *WAS GOD (*69). This GOD is *A
WAR GOD(*69).

*NORTH

*W or D

*SOUTH

THE FORMAT OF THE *NEWS(*61) *WORD(*60):

The Two Letters (o + r) in the Centre of the word, *W or D; is the 15th and 18th letter of the Roman Alphabet. Therefore:

$$1 + 5 = *6$$
$$1 + 8 = *9$$

The remaining two letters...(w + D) are Relative to the Two *inner (*60) letters of the *word (*60).

*W = 23 and 2+3 = *5
*D =....................= *4

The No: *54 is the *Chemical (*54) *Eclipse (*69) *of its (*69) *Blood Cycle (*96).

EXAMPLE:
$$6 \times 9 = *54$$
$$6 + 9 = \underline{*15}$$
       *69(*Message/*Essay/*His Name/*Worded/*A bad NEWS).

The letter *W and D* have the ability *TO PULL (*96) any *WORDED-CODE (*96) *INTO BALANCE (*96) *WITH OHM (*96) *OF ITS (*69) *MAGNET-FIELD (*96). This may very well be attributed to its *A.C./D.C characteristics pertaining to, inter alia:

   a) *Alternating Current = *220 = *Bi-directional Current *>-+<* = *Equilateral Current.

   b) Direct Current =*158 = *North + South)

   c)Alternating-Direct Current =*279 = *The Symbol of Sixty Nine/*The Symbol of Ninety-Six.*The Cross of Jesus Christ/*The Symbol of Chemical-Reaction.

NOTAS:

W	or	D
23		4

If the *NEWS IMAGE (*96) is an *ATOMIC-IMAGE (*96), then *W.E (**West and East) have a serious problem on our hands.

For it means that what *WE are now reading as *Daily (*51) NEWS (*61) is nothing more than the;

*Chemical Reaction of *51 + *61 =*122 =*West + EAST (*122).

Please note the following Characteristics of *A.C./D.C. in terms of the first and Last letters of the word, *WorD. As soon as you *Sever (*69) a *Worded Word (*129), you sever *Holy Text (*129). This causes the *Inner field (*96) to collapse upon itself and *brings (*69) the two *outer (*79) letters *Into balance (*96) with one another.

>W D<

234 =*THE ELECTRICAL RESISTANCE
 432 =*THE ELECTRICAL RESISTANCE OF NORTH and SOUTH.
*666

A.C./D.C. *AFTER   =   50
          *CHRIST =   77
          *DEVIL   =   52
          *COMES   =   55
                     *234

SPLITTING WORDS:

a) *PRO (*49)-TEIN (*48)................................= PROTEIN.
b) *SEA (*25)-GULL (*52)..............................= SEAGULL.
c) *UN (*35)-HEARD (*36)............................ = UNHEARD.
d) *WOOD (*57)-BORER (*58)......................= WOODBORER.
e) *SUR (*58)-PLUS (*68)............................ = SURPLUS.
f) *RE (*23)-MAND (*32)............................ = REMAND.
g) *MAN (*28)-KIND (*38)............................ = MANKIND.
h) *DUAL (*38)-MAN (*28)........................... = DUALMAN.
i) *WO (*38)-MAN (*28).............................. = WOMAN.
j) *PRO (*49)-GRAM (*39)........................... = PROGRAM.
k) *PHO (*39)-TON (*49)............................ = PHOTON.
l) *META (*39)-PHYSICAL (*93)................... = METAPHYSICAL.
m)*LAND (*31)-ING (*30)............................ = LANDING.
n) *SHIP (*52)-MENT (*52)........................... = SHIPMENT.
o) *CAR (*22)-GO (*22)................................ = CARGO.
p) *PRO (*49)-PHET (*49)............................ = PROPHET.
q) *HIPPO (*64)-CRATIC (*54)-OATH (*44)...... = HIPPOCRATIC OATH.
r) *DATE (*30)-LINE (*40)............................= DATELINE.
s) *GEAR (*31)-BOX (*41).............................. = GEARBOX.
t) *GUN (*42)-MEN (*32)...............................= GUNMEN.
u) *FREE (*34)-LANCE (*35)........................... = FREELANCE.
v) *MIND (*40)-KEY (*41).............................. = MINDKEY.
w)*DIS (*32)-ARM (*32)................................ = DISARM.
x) *DAILY (*51)-NEWS (*61)............................ = DAILYNEWS.
y) *DEAD (*14)-LOCK (*41)............................ = DEADLOCK.
z) *DEAD (*14)-KEY (*41)............................. = DEADKEY.

NOTAS:

In the following examples, you will see how words jump around each other, as well as being totally ***Ostracised** from the relationship shared by the other remaining words within the given sentence. All words that are *Ostracised...is/are indicated by an <u>underline</u>.

SPLITTING SENTENCE(S):

*A HARMONIC (*82) -*RHYTHM (*92)

1)

*LET (*37)... <u>the</u> *ANIMAL (*50) *INSIDE (*60) *YOU (*61). >= 37+36; 50+60; 60+61; 56+65.
*COME (*36) *OUT (*56) *TODAY (*65).

1b)

*COME-LET (*73) *THE ANIMAL (*83)   >=73+83; 60+61; 56+65.
*INSIDE (*60) *YOU (*61)
*OUT (*56) *TODAY (*65).

NOTE: In No:1, the word ***The** is omitted.
            In No:1b, the word ***The** is included.

2)

*LOOKING (*83) *DEATH (*38) <u>in</u> *THE FACE (*48)   >= 83+38, 38+48

3)

*ROCKET (*72) *FLYING (*73)   >= 72+73; 73+73; 73+74
*AROUND (*73) *IN A CIRCLE (*74)

4)

*ALIEN-MAN (*69) *SPACE-SHIP (*96)   >=69+96; 96+96; 96+69
*FLYING IN (*96) *CIRCLES (*69)

5)

*I am the Living bible (*159) *Whoever reads me (*161)   >=159+160+161...alternating.
*Will Live because.... (*160) *Of the Living Life... (*159)
*Within each word (*160) *That is of NEWS (*159).

6)

*HIS NAME (*69) *LIVES ON (*96) *THE COVER (*96) >=69+96; 96+97;97+98...alternating.
*OF ITS (*69) *STORY (*97) *AND WORDS (*98)
*IN BETWEEN (*97) *THE RECORD (*96).

7)

*DAILY (*51) *NEWS (*61)
*GOING (*52) *FULL (*51) *CIRCLE (*50)   >=51+61; 52+51+50
*FROM (*52) *ROME (*51)

8)

*MOVIES (*83).........*FOR (*39)   >=83+83; 83+38; 39+38
*SOUTH (*83)...*AFRICA (*38)

9)

*JACKIE CHAN (*65)... *FIGHTS (*69)   >=65+69;72+72+62;59+69;40+50;82+72
*FOR THE (*72) *WORLD (*72) *ACTION (*62)
*IN HIS (*59) *BIGGEST (*69)
*FILM (*40) *EVER (*50)
*STRIKE (*82) *FIRST (*72).
* DOG-PEDIGREE (*FOXES (*69) & *WOLVES (*96).

NOTE: There is no difference between *65 and *69, as they both have the same ***Numeric**
              No:*65 is the *Wolf(*56) dressed-up in *WOOL *WOOL

10)

* ACT NOT (*73) *UP TO (*72)   >73+72: 72+72
* WORLD (*72) *SCRATCH (*72).

11)

*SHOW ME (*83) *THE WAY (*82)   >=83+82; 32+42...'"to" is omitted.
to *GET (*32) *A HOME (*42).

NOTAS:

The same NUMERICAL RHYTHM is applicable to Names, Surnames and Proper names. As well as everything that can be *ASSOCIATED (*96) with *HIS NAME (*69) or the *CRAFT OF (*69) *IT"S TRADE (*96). If this is not *THE GENETIC (*96) of *A REAL LIFE (*69).... then please demonstrate anything in this World of ours, that is more *REALISTIC (*96) than this *TEXT (*69).

1) *DOCTOR (*75) *CHRIS (*57) *BARNARD (*58)   >=75+57; 57+58
a) *THE HEART (*85) *DOCTOR (*75)   >=85+75
b) *PATIENT (*85) *DOCTOR (*75)   >=85+75
c) *HEART (*52) *VALVE (*62)   >=52+62
d) *HEART-VALVE (*114) *SPECIALIST (*113)   >=114+113
e) *YIN AND YANG (*114) *SIX AND NINE (*113)   >=114+113

NOTAS: By now you should have the Rhythm of my ***message...*to you!**

2) *JOHN (*47) *MAJOR (*57)
a) *JOHN (*47) & *TONY (*74)
b) *MARGARET (*83) *THATCHER (*83)
c) *UNITED (*73) *KINGDOM (*73)
d) *PRINCE (*65) *CHARLES (*66)
e) *PRINCE (*65) *ANDREW (*65)
 f) *LADY DI (*55) & *CHARLES (*66)
g) *CHARLES (*66) & *ANDREW (*65)
h) *LADY (*42) *MAC BETH (*52)
i) *UNCLE (*55) *CHARLIE (*56)

*A HIERARCHY...*OF CRIME.

If there is 'one' lesson we learn well from History... is that we have learnt nothing from it; even though many have stated that History repeats itself on a line of continuity. For the past eighteen years, I have dedicated my life in search of this so-called "Historical Repetition". I started my research from Rome. As all roads lead to Rome, so too, must the same roads lead out of Rome. It was on this Point-in-Time that I caught-up with History, and followed ' IT' like the Night follows the Sun.

In order to understand the Harmonic Rhythm, One must first understand **The Matrix** (118). As all things in Nature can be expressed in terms of **The Matrix.** The design is to facilitate your understanding of it's Harmonic Rhythm. Once you understand it's format, you should be able to fully understand **The Dance of the Electron** (*206) (*The Dance of the Numbers).

The First **Ten Matrix** (*124) from Zero to Ten, as demonstrated to you under the first Law of Numerology, is what Science Has been playing around with in terms of basic-tools. (Ref: Calculators and Telephones Number order). Although The Matrix does extend itself beyond infinity, I have chosen to display its Numerical-dance up to the Numerical value of *99, only! To go beyond this value at this point of learning may cause complications to your understanding.

In a much later volume, I shall continue with its value to a much further extent. However, I do extend its value in *RELATIVE MATRIX. It is very important for the student of **GONTIERISM** to be fully conversant with the above **Matrix** in order to understand **RELATIVE MATRIX (THE DANCE OF THE MATRIX).**

RELATIVE MATRIX
*Biological Rhythm

Although It is the Relative of *RELATIVITY; it surpasses Albert Einstein's understanding of the subject, as it does not clothe itself as a sheep in wolves clothing; nor does it restrict itself to scientific logos perverted beyond its own definitions of mathematical correctness.

There is no such thing as**: Scientific Truth**. Science was never designed to show the path of Truth. It was designed to mislead the masses who went in search of Truth. Those who claim to be Experts in any given field...are all suffering from **Delusions of Grandeur**.

In my Life-Long search of Truth, I have gone in search of one person who could show me the truth of his or her understanding in terms of their so-called field of expertise. Up until now, I am still seeking that "one person".

The RELATIVE MATRIX is the Language of The Master's Archive. It defines all words in terms of its poetic and mathematical relationship in strict terms of ***RELATIVE MATRIX.**

AIR = 28	ANGEL = 39	APARTHEID = 82
LEAK = 29	of DEATH = 38	GOD'S LAW = 81
AIR = 28	ACTION = 62	A SECRET LORE = 121
MAN = 28	WHEELS = 72	REVELATION = 121
AIR = 28	A RIGHT = 63	ARABIC = 34
BASE = 27	WING = 53	MASK = 44
AIR = 28	ADAM KADMON = 77	AUTO = 57
GAS = 27	HUMAN EGG = 76	GLASS = 58
AIR = 28	ADAM KADMON = 77	AFRICAN = 52
A VACUUM = 82	HUMAN D.N.A. = 76	FIASCO = 53
AIR = 28	ASTRAL = 71	ARABIC = 34
STRIP = 82	SHADOW = 70	FACES = 34
ALPHA = 38	ASSAULT = 93	ADAM KADMON = 77
NUMERIC = 83	WEAPONS = 93	DUAL-MAN = 66
AMERICAN = 64	AMERICAN = 64	AMAZON = 70
CROSS = 74	HERO = 46	JUNGLE = 69
AFTER = 50	ANCIENT = 66	AUTO = 57
BEFORE = 51	GREEKS = 65	CRATE = 47
ACID = 17	ANCIENT = 66	AUTOCRACY = 107
HEAD = 18	MASTER = 76	MILITARY = 107
AIR = 28	ANCIENT = 66	ATOMIC-AGE = 74
BALANCE = 38	ARCHIVE = 66	NUCLEAR = 74
ALCHEMY = 67	ANGLICAN = 61	ALKALI = 46
CHEMIST = 77	CHURCH = 61	BASES = 46
ALCOHOL = 66	ANGLICAN = 61	ASTRONOMERS = 157
ETHER= 56	CATHOLIC = 71	STAR OF BETHLEHEM = 157
ABSTRACT = 84	ALTERED = 65	ABSOLUTE = 95
CONCRETE = 83	STATE = 65	KNOWLEDGE = 96
ALARM = 45	ANIMALS = 69	AUTO = 57
CLOCK = 44	VEGETABLE = 79	NOMY = 58
ANUS = 55	AUTO = 57	A PHOTO = 75
SHIT = 56	MOBILE = 56	FINISH = 65
ADAM'S = 38	AFRICAN = 52	AFRICANISM = 93
SIDE = 37	DEFENCE = 42	TRIBALISM = 103
ACCIDENT = 59	AFRICAN = 52	ATOMIC SCIENCE = 119
CRASH = 49	KAFFIR = 51	SCIENCE OF MIND = 119
ALPHA AND OMEGA = 98	AFRIKAANS = 80	A BRIGHTER = 88
CROSSES = 98	ZULU = 80	VISION = 88
AIR = 28	AUTO = 57	AUNT = 56
STRIKE = 82	BOUND = 56	UNCLE = 55
ALPHA-BETA = 66	ANIMALS = 69	AIR WAYS = 96
ALPHABET = 65	VEGETABLE = 79	PORT = 69
ARE = 24	ANIMALS = 69	AIR-WAVES = 98
ONE = 34	PEOPLE = 69	AIR-PORT = 97
ADAM AND EVE = 70	A KNOCK = 55	A WHITE BEARD = 96
MOM AND DAD = 69	OUT = 56	HO-HO-HO = 69

AFRICAN = 52
TRIBAL = 62

A PLUS (+) = 69
AND A MINUS (-) = 96

B

BANK = 28
BALANCE =38

BLACK = 29
BELT = 39

BACILLUS = 79
PROTEIN = 97

BORN = 49
THIEF = 48

BEAUTY = 74
BEAST = 47

BEST = 46
FRIEND = 5

BACILLUS = 79
VIRUS = 89

BEE-SHIT = 68
HONEY = 67

BETTER = 70
WORSE = 80

BLACK = 29
DOT = 39

BURIED = 59
ALIVE = 49

BONUS = 71
MONEY = 72

BORN = 49
WILD = 48

BASE = 27
BALL = 27

BRIGHT = 64
SPARK = 65

BOXING = 71
WORLD = 72

BUY = 48
SELL = 48

BEST = 46
TI ME = 47

BRITISH = 85
CITIZEN = 86

BRIGHT = 64
SUN = 54

BLACK & WHITE = 94

COLOURED = 93

BRITISH = 85
GENTLEMEN = 95

EUROPEAN = 95
GENTLEMEN = 85

BLACK & WHITE = 94
COLOUR = 84

BULLET = 72
TRAIN = 62

BLACK-BALL = 56
CUE-BALL = 56

BOUNCING = 85
PARTICLE = 84

BOUNCED = 64
ENERGY = 74

BRUTAL = 74
FORCE = 47

BABY TALK = 74
DIALOGUE = 74

BIONIC = 52
HEART = 52

BIONIC = 52
HEARING = 62

BLAZE = 46
LIGHT = 56

BRIDESMAID = 84
BRIDESMAN = 85

BANK-RATE = 72
MONEY = 72

BLUE = 40
JEAN = 30

BLACK CAT = 53
WITCH = 63

BRAKE = 37
FORCE = 47

BRAKE = 37
DANCE = 27

BALL = 27
DANCE = 27

BEST = 46
FOOT = 56

BRIAN'S = 63
CIRCUS = 73

BALL = 27
GAME = 26

BRILLIANT = 97

KNOWLEDGE = 96

BUSINESS COMPANY = 195
THE HIPPO CRATIC OATH = 195

C

COSMIC = 62
RAYS = 63

CUPID = 53
LOVE = 54

CROSS = 74
ARROW = 75

CHARTS = 69
ROUTE = 79

CORNER = 73
STONE = 73

CRITICAL = 75
POINT = 74

CHEMICAL REACTION = 139
FERMENTATION = 140

COMPUTER BRAIN = 155
MICRO SOFT-WARE = 165

CATHOLIC = 71
CHURCH = 61

CATHOLIC = 71
PARISH = 71

CATHOLIC = 71
POPES = 71

CLOSED = 58
OPENED = 59

CHILDREN = 73
PARENT = 74

COW = 41
BOY = 42

COW = 41
BITCH = 42

COOL = 45
WARM = 55

CAR ACCIDENT = 81
CAR CRASH = 71

CRAWL = 57
WALK = 47

CAPTAIN = 64
SAILOR = 74

CLEAR = 39
MIND = 40

COSMIC = 62
WORLD = 72

COSMIC = 62
EARTH = 52

CALCULATE = 78
WORDS = 79

CALCULATE = 78
ALPHA & OMEGA = 79

CELL-MUTATION = 145
PROTOPLASM = 145

CHANGES = 57
TIME = 47

CAUSES = 68
MOTION = 86

CONSCIOUS BEING = 155
DIVINE PRINCIPLE = 165

CONSCIOUS BEING = 155
GODLY PRINCIPLE = 165

CENTRAL MONAD = 120
STAR OF DAVID = 119

CENTRAL TIME = 120
SCIENCE OF MIND = 119

COLOUR = 84
OF RIGHT = 83

COLOUR = 84
ENERGY = 74

CORPOREAL WORLD = 175
WEST MEETS EAST = 174

CUT = 44
TEAR = 44

CAR-DRIVE = 80
DRIVER = 81

CRIME = 48
TIME = 47

CREDIT = 59
RATING = 69

CODEX-NASARAEUS = 150
THE DEAD SEA SCROLL = 151

CODEX-NASARAEUS = 150
ALPHABETICAL ORDER = 150

COAT = 39
HAT = 29

CITY = 57
FATHER = 58

CHICKENS = 72
COUNT = 73

COUNT = 73

MONEY = 72
CHANGE IN NATURE = 140
CHEMICAL REACTION = 139

CANON = 47
BALLS = 46

CANON = 47
TIME = 47

CHICKEN = 53
GOAT = 43

SHEEP = 53
GOAT = 43
CALCULATION = 111
MATHEMATICS = 112

COMPUTER = 111
MATHEMATICS = 112

COINING = 71
MONEY = 72

CARPET = 63
GRASS = 64

CAR = 22
GO = 22

CIRCLE = 50
OVAL = 50

CROSS = 74
COLOUR = 84

CREATION = 85
GOD FATHER = 84

CANDLE = 39
FIRE = 38

BLACK & WHITE = 94
COLOURED = 93

CRIMINALS = 98
THIEVES = 88

CRIMINALS = 98
POLICEMAN = 88

COUNT-DOWN = 129
JUDGEMENT-DAY = 129

CHESS = 54
GAMES = 45

CHECK-MATE = 69
STALE-MATE = 96

CASTLE = 60
ROOK = 59

CASTLES = 79
KNIGHT = 69

CASTLES = 79
BISHOP = 69

COCK = 32
TAIL = 42

CARTOON = 86
CHARACTERS = 96

CAVE = 31
MEN = 32

CON = 32
CAVE = 31

CLONE = 49
FOETAL = 59

CLOSED = 58
SHUT = 68
COURT = 77
JUSTICE = 88

COURTS = 96
CHAMBERS = 69

CHAMBERS = 69
TOMBS = 69

CASKET = 59
TOMBS = 69

CITIZEN = 86
BUREAU = 68

CLIP = 40
BOARD = 40

CIVIL WAR = 97
CONTROL = 97

CHICKEN = 53
RUN = 53

CHUCKED = 55
OUT = 56

CHAOS = 46
RULE = 56

CHUCK = 46
OUT = 56

CHILDS = 55
PLAY = 54

COMPUTER = 111
PROGRAMER = 111

CRACK = 36
BREAK = 37

CODE = 27
BREAK = 37

COAL = 31
BOX = 41

COSATU = 79
POPCRU = 89

COSATU = 79
BOSSES = 79

COSATU = 79
LABOUR = 69

COMPANY = 87
CONTROL = 97

CONTROL = 97
NOTHING = 87

CITY = 57
GHETTO = 75

COMPUTER MIND = 151
RELATIVITY = 141

CLOCK = 44
ONE = 34

CLOCK = 44
ALARM = 45

CHIEF = 31
KING = 41

CASH = 31
KING = 41

CHICKEN = 53
FEATHER = 63

CRUCIFIED = 78
CHRIST = 77

CHRIST = 77
ADAM KADMON = 77

CAIN AND ABEL = 66
DUAL-MAN = 66

CHRIST = 77
THE GOD-HEAD = 77

CRYPTICISM = 135
THE FACTS OF LIFE = 135

CRYPTICISM = 135
NUMEROLOGY = 145

CHILD'S = 55
PLAY = 54

CHEQUE = 59
WEALTH = 69

CODE OF CONDUCT = 128
HOLLYWOOD = 129

CHEMICAL = 54
PATH = 45

CAMERA = 41
FILM = 40

CLAY = 41
POT = 51

CASINO = 61
CHURCH = 61

CAST = 43
LOOK = 53

CROW = 59
NEST = 58

CONDOM = 64
PENIS = 63

COUNT-DOWN = 129
JUDGEMENT-DAY = 129

COUNT-DOWN = 129
PANDORA'S BOX = 129

CHAOTIC = 59
ORDER = 60

CORNER = 73
STONE = 73

CARDS = 45
CHESS = 54

CELIBACY = 60
VOW = 60

CELIBATED = 61
CELIBACY = 60

CELIBATED = 61
HOMO = 51

CROSS = 74
EXAMINED = 75

COP = 34
EYE = 35

COP = 34
IMAGE = 35

COSTUME = 96
UNIFORM = 96

COWARD = 64
HERO = 46

CRY = 46
WOLF = 56

CITIZEN = 86
SOCIETY = 96

CITIZEN = 86
DENIZENS = 96

CONJUGATE = 96
UNITE = 69

CONJUGATION = 129
GONTIERISM = 129

CUPID = 53
ARCHER = 53

CUPID = 53
LOVE = 54

CAMELOT = 69
KNIGHT = 69

CATHARS = 70
KNIGHT = 69

CLONING = 74
CHILDREN = 73

CLONING = 74
PARENT = 74

COMPU = 68
SERVE = 69

CELESTIAL-WORLD = 158
PYRAMID-WORLD = 158

COMPUTER-BRAIN = 155
MICRO-SOFT-WARE = 165

COMPUTER-MIND = 151
JESUS CHRIST = 151

CROWDED = 72
WORLD = 72

CEMENT = 60
LATTICE = 70

CITY = 57
ANGELS = 58

D

DISEASE = 62
MEDICINE = 62

DEVILS = 71
ADVOCATE = 71

DRUG = 50
LORD = 49

DOUBLE = 59
HELIX = 58

DIAMETER = 75
POINT = 74

DIAMETER = 75
CROSS = 74

DOOR = 52
KNOB = 42

DEATH = 38
HADES = 37

DEATH = 38
HELL = 37

DEFINITE = 72
LIMITS = 82

DEGREE = 44

PATH = 45	KEY = 41	SQUAD = 62
DANCING = 52	DALAI = 26	DREAM = 41
DEVIL = 52	LAMA = 27	GOOD = 41
DIGITS = 68	DIAMETER = 75	DROPS = 72
FINGERS = 78	CENTER = 65	UNDER = 62
DONKEY = 74	DIAMETER = 75	DISNEY = 76
THE CART = 75	ORIFICE = 65	CARTOON = 86
DEMOCRACY = 87	DIS = 32	DIGI = 29
SLAVES = 78	CHARGE = 42	NET = 39
DEMOCRAT = 79	DOG = 26	DAY DREAM = 71
SLAVES = 78	STICK = 62	I THINK = 71
DEMOCRATIC = 91	DOG = 26	DAILY = 51
MESSIANIC = 92	BONE = 36	NEWS = 61
DEMOCRATS = 98	DISTANCE = 75	DELIVERER = 98
THE WOLF = 89	DIAMETER = 75	DELIVERANCE = 98
DEVIL = 52	DOLLAR = 62	DELIVERANCE = 98
PAPACY = 62	MONEY = 72	JUDGEMENT = 99
DEVIL = 52	DOLLAR = 62	DRUG = 50
REST = 62	CAPITAL = 62	FOOD = 40
DOOR = 52	DRUGS = 69	DOWN = 56
LADY = 42	MARKET = 68	UPS = 56
DURBAN = 60	DIVORCE = 76	DOUBLE = 59
HEROES = 70	MARRY = 75	MINDED = 49
DARRELL GONTIER = 158	DEATH = 38	DIE HOND = 58
HUMAN COMPUTER = 158	SEAL = 37	THE DOG = 59
DOS = 38	DIVIDED DNA = 76	DOPE = 40
MODE = 37	THE GOD HEAD = 77	DRUG = 50
DELEGATE = 59	DEFENCE = 42	DOOD = 38
DRAFTED = 58	SELF = 42	DEATH = 38
DOUGH = 55	DEBTH = 39	DUCK = 39
NUT = 55	DEATH = 38	POND = 49
DRAFT = 49	DATA = 26	DEEP = 30
DELEGATE = 59	BASE = 27	MIND = 40
DURBAN = 60	DATA = 26	DANGER = 49
BOYS = 61	CODE = 27	SIGN = 49
DRIVE OFF = 85	DIGIT = 49	DUPLICATED = 95
DRIVE BACK = 75	DOT = 39	COPY = 59
DNA = 19	DIS-= 32	DIVINE = 63
GROWTH = 91	ARM = 32	LEGACY = 53
DISCONNECT = 106	DRUGS = 69	DEMON = 51
THE CROWD = 96	CARTEL = 59	DEVIL = 52
DEVIL = 52	DIRTY = 76	DEMONIC MAGIC = 96
POPE = 52	MATTER = 77	SATANISM = 96
DEAD = 14	DIRTY = 76	DENIZENS = 96
LOCK = 41	WATER = 77	CITIZEN = 86
DEAD = 14	DOG = 26	DOCTOR = 75

WHITE = 65

DOCTOR = 75
VETERAN = 85

DEFENDING = 68
THE LAW = 69

DRAW = 46
BRIDGE = 45

DWARF = 52
GIANT = 51

D JA VU = 63
FLASH BACK = 63

DEVELOPMENT = 131
THE ALPHA AND OMEGA = 131

DEVELOP = 79
NATURE = 79

DEVELOPED = 88
VISION = 88

DESK = 39
TABLE = 40

DESK = 39
CHAIR = 39

DOWN = 56
OUT = 56

DOWN HERE = 92
UP THERE = 93

DIRKIE = 56
UYS = 65

DECIMAL = 47
POINT = 74

E

EYE = 35
LOOK = 53

EYE = 35
IMAGE = 35

EYE = 35
NOSE = 53

EARTH = 52
AXIS = 53

ENGINEERS = 96
ARCHITECT = 106

ENDLESS = 78
YEARS = 68

ELECTRIC = 75
ENERGY = 74

ELECTRICITY = 129
GONTIERISM = 129

ENDS = 42
MEET = 43

EYE = 35
CAMEL = 34

EYE = 35
LID = 25

ELECTRO = 78
DYNAMICS = 88

EARTH = 52
GRAVE = 53

EGG = 19
HEAD = 18

ECONOMICS = 96
EQUITY = 97

CONTROL = 97
FREEMASON = 96

ECONOMICS = 96
WEALTH = 69

EGO = 27
MAN = 28

ETYMOLOGY = 137
SYMBOLISM = 127

ELEPHANT = 81
TUSK = 71

ENGINE = 54
MACHINE = 53

ELECTRICAL = 88
CROSSES = 98

ENERGY = 74
SOUND = 73

ENERGY = 74
TIME = 74

ENERGY = 74
MOVES = 74

ESCOM'S = 74
NUCLEAR = 74
ESCOM'S = 74
ELECTRIC = 75

ELECTRIC = 75
CITY = 57

EMBRYO = 78
GENESIS = 78

EMBRYO = 78
CLONES = 68

EMBRYO = 78
MOTHER = 79

EMPIRICAL = 86
KNOWLEDGE = 96

ETHER = 56
LIGHT = 56

ENERGY = 74
SCREEN = 64

ELECTRON = 92
MEASURE = 82

ETHEREAL = 74
ENERGY = 74

ESSENCE = 70
THE LAW = 69

ELECTRO-MAGNETIC-ETHER = 206
THE MAGNET RESISTANCE = 206

ELECTRO-MAGNETIC-ETHER = 206
YOUR MIRROR IMAGE = 205

ENLIGHTENMENT = 146
ILLUMINATIVE = 147

EX- = 29
TRA = 39

ELI-ELI LAMA = 79
SABACHTANI = 78

ENGLISH = 74
SPEAKER = 75

EMPLOY = 86
EMPLOYEE = 96

EYE= 35
LOG = 34

EXPERTISM = 129
BEGOTTEN-KEY = 129

ENTERTAINMENT = 158
NORTH SOUTH = 158

EVENING = 76
STARS = 77

EUROPEAN = 95
KNOWLEDGE = 96

EUROPEAN = 95
BRITISH = 85

EGYPTIAN = 97
KNOWLEDGE = 96

ELEPHANT = 81
TUSK = 71

ENERGY DEN = 97
CEREBELLUM = 96

EMPORER = 90
SELASSIE = 89

ENTERTAINER = 129
HOLLYWOOD = 129

ETHIOPIA = 83
JAMAICA = 38

ETHIOPIAN = 97
A CITIZEN = 87

EAGLE = 30
LANDED = 40

ENJOYS = 88
ENJOYED = 78

EMERGING = 78
MARKET = 68

EXTRA = 68
TWO = 58

EXPANDING = 94
ZERO = 64

ESOTERIC = 94
THIRD EYE= 94

EYE = 35
LID = 25

F

FAMOUS PEOPLE = 144
FIRST AND LAST = 143

FAMOUS PEOPLE = 144
LIFE MUTATION = 145

FOOD = 40
TABLE = 40

FUNGUS = 88
PARASITE = 89

FREEDOM = 66
SONG = 55

FREQUENCIES = 122
EIGHTY-EIGHT = 123

FREQUENCY = 114
YING AND YANG = 114

FREEMASONARY = 139
HOLLYWOOD = 129

FREQUENCY = 114
SIX AND NINE = 113

FIRST = 72
COUPLE = 72

FELO DE SE = 71
SUICIDE = 70

FANATIC = 54
ISLAM = 54

FANATICISM = 95

MOSLEMS = 96

FOCUS = 64
POINT = 74

FAMILY = 66
FRIEND = 56

FALLEN = 50
LOW = 50

FREEDOM = 66
SPEECH = 56

FINGER = 59
READING = 58

FAST = 46
LIGHT = 56

FIRE = 38
CALL = 28

FIRE = 38
AIR = 28

FIRE = 38
MAN = 28

FIRE = 38
TEAM = 39

FIRE = 38
& HELL = 37

FIRE = 38
& HADES = 37

FIRES = 57
ARSON = 67

FIRING = 63
SQUAD = 62

FISH = 42
LIFE = 32

FISH = 42
BAIT = 32

FISH = 42
MEN = 32

FISH = 42
SHIP = 42

FISHING = 72
SCHOOL = 72

FATHER = 58
SON = 48

FLASH = 46
LIGHT = 56

FIRST = 72
SHOT = 62

FLASH = 46

TORCH = 64

FULL = 51
CIRCLE = 50

FLOW = 56
TIDES = 57

FLOTSAM = 86
JETSAM = 68

FIELD = 36
RAYS = 63

FRESH = 56
STALE = 57

FLYING = 73
OBJECTS = 74

FORMER = 75
LATTER = 76

FIRE = 38
& BLOOD = 48

FIVE = 42
SIX = 52

FUSION = 84
ENERGY = 74

FIRED = 42
GUN = 42

FLUSH = 66
WATER = 67

FLUSH = 66
SHIT = 56

FLUSH = 66
URINE = 67

FIRST = 72
FELLOW = 73

FAT LADY = 69
FAT BOY = 69

FAT LADY = 69
SINGS = 68

FAT-LADY = 69
FAT WHORE = 96

FAT-BOY = 69
PLAY-BOY = 96

FAGGOT = 56
QUEER = 66

FAGGOT = 56
JUDGES = 66

FAGGOT = 56
DUAL-MAN = 66

FIBRE-GLASS = 98

WINDOW = 88

FLAT = 39
MATE = 39

FORT NAPIER = 122
FORT KNOX = 123

FLY = 43
RUN = 53

FIRST = 72
NUMBER = 73

FIRST = 72
WORLD = 72

FIRE = 38
SIDE = 37

FIRE = 38
PLACE = 37

FIRE = 38
ASH = 28

FURTHER = 96
KNOWLEDGE = 96

FREEMASON = 96
JUDICIAL CODE = 96

FREEMASON = 96
ITALIAN MAFIA = 96

FLESH = 50
WINE = 51

FUTURE-WATCH = 146
NOSTRADAMUS = 145

FAST = 46
LIGHT = 56

FAST = 46
FLASH = 46

FERTILE = 75
CENTRE = 65

FILM-STAR = 98
FILM-IDOLS = 99

FRESH = 56
FORCES = 66

FIXED = 48
TIME = 47

FORT = 59
NIGHT = 58

FISH-LINE = 82
FISH-NET = 81

FOOLS = 67
RUSH = 66

FOOL = 48

GOLD = 38

FIRST = 72
HOST = 62

FREE = 34
CHOICE = 43

FAMILY = 66
JEWEL = 55

FIRE = 38
FLAME = 37

FIRE = 38
CANDLE = 39

FREE = 34
LANCE = 35

FREE-LANCE = 69
CAMERA-MAN = 69

FREE-LANCE = 69
RED-TAPE = 69

FREE-LANCE CODE = 96
NEWS-IMAGE = 96

FREE-LANCE = 69
TEXT = 69

FISHES = 66
WATER = 67

FISHES = 66
MEDIUM = 65

FISHES = 66
DUAL-MAN = 66

FISHES = 66
WO-MAN = 66

FISHES = 66
MAN-KIND = 66

FISHES = 66
CAIN AND ABEL = 66

FLAME = 37
OIL = 36

FORE = 44
PLAY = 54

FASHION = 72
CLOTHES = 82

FASHION = 72
SEXUAL = 82

FOREHEAD = 81
TEMPLE = 71

FASHION = 72
WORLD = 82

FASHION = 72

SCHOOL = 72

FASHION = 72
MONEY = 72

FRONT = 73
SCHOOL = 72

FISH = 42
TIN = 43

FULL = 51
VALUE = 61

FULL = 51
PRICE = 51

FISH MEETS FISH = 146
THE YIN AND YANG = 147

FOR HIM = 69
& FOR HER = 70

FRUIT = 74
SEASON = 73

FOOT-BALL = 83
CLUB = 38

G

GAS = 27
FLAME = 37

GRANNY = 79
OUMAS = 69

GRANNY = 79
MOTHER = 79

GRANNY = 79
SMITH = 69

GRANNY = 79
APPLES = 69

GRANNY = 79
GRUNDY = 89

GOD = 26
GOTT = 62

GENESIS = 78
THE GOD HEAD = 77

GENESIS = 78
START = 78

GENESIS = 78
ONE GOD-HEAD = 78

GOD-FATHER = 84
GOD-SON = 74

GOD'S IMAGE = 80
ALPHA & OMEGA = 79

GREATER = 74
SACRIFICE = 73

GREATER = 74
NUMBER = 73

GHOST = 69
HOUSE = 68

GHOST = 69
TOMBS = 69

GHOST = 69
VIRGIN = 79

GIRL = 46
FRIEND = 56

GREEN = 49
APPLE = 50

GREEN = 49
TREE = 48

GREEN = 49
BLOOD = 48

GOLDEN = 57
THREAD = 56

GOLDEN = 57
LIGHT = 56

GOLDEN = 57
MOON = 57

GESTAPO = 83
THE NAZI = 83

GESTAPO = 83
SOLDIER = 82

GENETIC IN-BREEDING = 150
CODEX NASARAEUS = 150

GENETIC IN-BREEDING = 150
ELECTRO MAGNETIC = 150

GENETICS = 82
MARK OF RA = 83

GENETICS = 82
MARK OF ADAM = 83

GRAVE = 53
R. I. P. = 43

GRID = 38
NET = 39

GENETIC IN-BREEDING = 150
THE BIRTH OF MIND = 151

GUN = 42
MEN = 32

GUN = 42
WAR = 42

GUN = 42
COCK = 32

GRAVE = 53
MARK = 43

GOLDEN = 57
SILENCE = 67

GOD'S LIFE = 77
EXOTIC = 76

GOOD-LIFE = 73
NEW LIFE = 74

CRUCIFIED = 78
MURDER = 79

GAS = 27
AIR = 28

GENESIS = 78
GOD'S LIFE = 77

GENESIS = 78
GOD AND LIFE = 77

GENESIS = 78
NIRVANA = 79

GATE = 33
FENCE = 33

GOD = 26
QUEEN = 62

GEAR = 31
LOCK = 41

GEAR = 31
BOX = 41

GEAR = 31
KEY = 41

GEAR-CHANGE = 69
BAR-RING = 69

GEAR-CHANGE = 69
THE RATIO = 96

GLOBAL = 49
VIEW = 59

GOATS = 43
KIDS = 43

GOAT = 43
SHEEP = 53

GREEN = 49
BERET = 50

GOLD = 38
FOOL = 48

GRID-LOCK = 79
WWW = 69

GRID-LOCK = 79
WEB-NET = 69

GRID-LOCK = 79
GRID-KEY = 79

GRID-LOCK = 79
NET-HOLE = 79

GLOW = 57
MOON = 56

GLOWING = 87
MATTER = 77

GOD = 26
SAKE = 36

GENERAL = 62
PUBLIC = 63

GRAVE = 53
SITE = 53

GRAVE = 53
WOMB = 53

GOLDEN = 57
SPEECH = 56

GLOBAL = 49
TRADE = 48

GLASS = 58
WALL = 48

GLASS = 58
HOUSE = 68

GOOD = 41
BOY = 42

GIANT = 51
GREAT = 51

GIANT = 51
ADAM & EVE = 51

GOOD-MORNING = 131
SOUTH AFRICA = 121

GANGLION = 79
DRUGS = 69

GOLD = 38
RING = 48

GREEN = 49
FINGER = 59

GOVERNOR = 114
SIX AND NINE = 113

GOVERNMENT = 133
MARXIST DOGMA = 144

GOVERNMENT = 133
THE SKELETON = 134

GLASS = 58
TUBE = 48

GREEN = 49
CORN = 50

GREEN = 49
TOBACCO = 59

GLOBAL = 49
NET = 39

GLOBAL = 49
VIEW = 59

GREEN = 49
LAWN = 50

GURUS = 86
DISCIPLES = 96

GURU = 67
CHRIST = 77

H

HOT = 43
COLD = 34

HE = 13
HER = 31

HIM = 30
HER = 31

HYBRID = 66
COMBINED = 65

HERMIT = 73
RECLUSE = 83

HONEY = 67
MOON = 57

HYDRO = 70
DYNAMIC = 69

HILL = 41
HOLE = 40

HIS = 36
SIDE = 37

HERO = 46
COWARD = 64

HILL = 41
TOP = 51

HANDS = 46
FOOT = 56

HANDS = 46
FEET = 36

HIS = 36
HANDS = 46

HAND = 27
BALL = 27

HUMAN = 57
ZOO = 56

HAMMER = 58
SICKEL = 59

HOLD = 39
ON = 29

HARI KARI = 75
LIFE CUT = 76

HEART = 52
VALVE = 62

HOURS OF THE DAY = 165
THE ALPHA AND THE OMEGA = 164

HUMAN = 57
SOUL = 67

HEAT = 34
IMAGE = 35

HANDS = 46
FEELS = 47

HARD = 31
CASH = 31

HARD = 31
DAY = 30

HOW = 46
MUCH = 45

HEAVENLY BODIES = 146
INTERCOURSE = 147

HANDS = 46
TIME = 47

HOME = 41
LAND = 31

HOUSE = 68
WORK = 67

HIPPIES = 82
NARCOTIC = 83

HOMO = 51
RABBIT = 52

HOLY VEHM OF LIFE = 161
HIPPO-CRATIC-OATH = 162

HEADLESS = 73
CROSS = 74

HIPPO-CRATIC-OATH = 162
SECRET SACRIFICES = 162

HE = 13
DIED = 14

HEAD = 18
ACHE = 17

HUMAN = 57
TOUCH = 67

HURT = 67
TOUCH = 67

HOLLYWOOD = 129
TELEVISION = 130

HOUSE OF SOLOMON = 192
THE KEY OF KNOWLEDGE = 191

HOUSE = 68
PYRAMID = 86

THE EYE = 68
PYRAMID = 86

HOUND = 62
DOG = 26

HINDUISM = 97
KNOWLEDGE = 96

HEAVEN = 55
GODS = 45

HINDU = 56
SARIS = 66

HOT TEA = 69
SWEAT = 68

HEAVY = 61
METAL = 51

HAILE = 35
GERIMA = 53

HAIR = 36
WIG = 39

HARNESS = 84
ENERGY = 74

HAND = 27
UP = 37

HANDS = 46
DOWN = 56

HISPANIC = 79
NIGGERS = 79

HISTORY = 114
HISTORIAN = 113

HISTORIAN = 113
CONNECTION = 112

HIS SEED = 69
GROUND = 79

HITLER = 72
POLAND = 62

HIM = 30
MALE = 31

HUMAN = 57
FORCE = 47

HAND = 27
BREAK = 37

HOLD = 39
BIND = 29

HAMLET = 59
GHOST = 69

HIS LIFE = 68
HIS SEED = 69

HOUSES = 87
POWER = 77

HARMONISED MUSIC = 171
MELODIC MINOR SCALE = 170

HIT ROCK = 84
BOTTOM = 85

HEY = 38
MAN = 28

HORSE AND = 84
TRAILER = 83

HELP = 41
MOM = 41

HOT AIR = 71
BALLOON = 71

HEALTHIER = 86
CITIZEN = 86

HOLDING TEN COMMANDEMENTS =
242
THEORY OF GONTIERISM = 241

HE THINKS = 81
I THINK = 71

I

INK = 34
PEN = 35

IRON = 56
OXIDE = 57

IRON = 56
MAIDEN = 46

INSTANT = 97
KNOWLEDGE = 96

INTEGRATED = 103
CIRCUITS = 102

INFRA-RED = 75
ENERGY = 74

INCOM = 54
TAX = 45

IDENTICAL = 77
SPLIT = 76

INNATE IDEAS = 101
INNER SELF = 102

INSTANT = 97
CONTROL = 97

ISLAND = 59
PEOPLE = 69

IMMUTABLE = 96
THE LAW = 69

IGNITED BY = 95
THE BRAINS = 96

INTERMAP = 96
INTERWEB = 96

IMMORALITY ACT = 159
THE FORBIDDEN SEX = 158

I SPLIT MYSELF = 165
THE ALPHA AND OMEGA = 165

IRON = 56
BODY = 46

IMAGINATION = 112
THIRD EYES = 113

IMMOBILE = 78
MATTER = 77

INTER = 66
LUNAR = 66

INTELLIGENTSIA = 156
PATH TO GO TO RA = 156

IDEA = 19
HEAD = 18

ICE-CREAM = 57
CONES = 56

INTENSITY = 135
ELECTRICAL CYCLE = 136

INTER = 66
WEAVE = 56

INTER = 66
CITIES = 56

IDEAL = 31
ISM = 41

IMAGE = 35
LOOK = 53

ILLUMINATI = 120
BRIGHTNESS = 121

ILLUMINANT = 125
LUMINOUS = 124

ILLUMINATION = 149
ILLUTIONIST = 159

INTERFERENCE = 122
EIGHTY-EIGHT = 123

ISLAMIC = 66
LAWS = 55

IMPRISONMENT = 165
IMPRISON POPE = 164

I KNOW = 72
I THINK = 71

INCREASE = 74
DECREASED = 64

I'M TIRED = 78
ME TOO = 68

INTERNET = 105
ELECTRONIC = 104

J

JESUS = 74
JOSEPH = 73

JESUS = 74
JOHN = 47

JESUS = 74
PETER = 64

JOHN = 47
JAMES= 48

JAMES= 48
LUKE = 49

JAIL = 32
BIRD = 33

JUDGE = 47
JURY = 74

JUDGES = 66
GOOD AND BAD = 67

JESUS = 74
MESSIAH = 74

JESUS CHRIST = 151
HOLY SPIRIT = 151

JOHN = 47
SON = 48

JOB = 27
CARD = 26

JUDIASM = 77
KOSHER = 76

JESUS = 74
NAZARENE = 84

JESUS = 74

GOD-FATHER = 84

JESUS = 74
GOD-SON = 74

JUDGE = 47
LEGAL = 37

JESUS CHRIST = 151
THE NOBLE NAME OF GOD = 161

JESUS = 74
PERFECT = 73

JESUS CHRIST = 151
RELATIVITY = 141

JUSTICE = 87
STRIKED = 86

THE NOBLE NAME OF GOD = 161
THE ROOT OF DAVID = 162

JOHN = 47
DEERE = 37

JAYCEES = 68
LIONS = 69

JOHN = 47
BUCK = 37

JOHN = 47
MARY = 57

JONAH = 48
WHALE = 49

JUDGEMENT = 99
JUDGES = 66

JAPAN = 42
WAR = 42

JOIN = 48
CLUB = 38

JOSEPH = 73
SLOVO = 83

JEWISH = 74
GHETTO = 75

JUNK FOOD = 96
SHIT FOOD = 96

JUNK FOOD = 96
FAST FOOD = 86

JOSEPH = 73
FRAZER = 74

JOHN = 47
TATE = 46

JOURNAL = 91
NUMBERS = 92

JOURNALIST = 139

SIXTY NINE = 139
JOURNALIST = 139
GONTIERISM = 129

JOURNALISM = 132
TRIPLE SIX = 132

JOURNALISM = 132
THE ALPHA AND OMEGA = 131

JOURNALISM = 132
THE MAGNET BALANCE = 131

JESUS CHRIST = 151
THE NAME OF MY GOD = 151

JIMI HENDRIX = 123
TECHNOLOGY = 124

JUNE 6 DAY = 86
JUNE 16 DAY = 96

K

KILLING = 74
TIME = 47

KNIFE = 45
CUT = 44

KING = 41
DAVID = 40

KING DAVID = 81
PSALMS = 80

KING DAVID = 81
MIND KEY = 81

KNOWLEDGE = 96
HUMAN MIND = 97

KNOWLEDGE = 96
THE INNATE = 96

KING DAVID = 81
SAINTS = 82

KING DAVID = 81
THE FATHER = 91

KICK = 34
ARSE = 43

KING DAVID = 81
CREATOR = 80

KING DAVID = 81
SAMSON = 81

KING DAVID = 81
KING SHAKA = 81

KING SHAKA = 81
ZULU = 80

KAFFIRS = 70
ZULU = 80

KISS = 58
AND TELL = 68

KNOWLEDGE = 96
INSIGHT = 86

KARL MARX = 98
GOD HIMSELF = 98

KARL MARX = 98
PROPHET = 98

KARMA = 44
EFFECT = 45

KARMA = 44
FREE = 34

KODAK = 42
CAMERA = 41

KEY = 41
BOARD = 40

KEY = 41
DELTA = 42

KEMPTON = 94
PARK = 46

SILICONE 86
KNOWLEDGE = 96

KISS = 58
AND TELL = 68

KRUGER = 80
WILD LIFE = 80

KEEP UP WITH = 134
TECHNOLOGY = 124

KING = 41
FISH = 42

KNOWLEDGE = 96
COMPETES = 96

L

LEAK = 29
LAKE = 29

LOVE = 54
SONG = 55

LIGHT = 56
CENTRE = 65

LABOUR = 69
MARKET = 69

LOOP = 58
HOLES = 59

LOOK = 53
SIGHT = 63

LOOK = 53	LAWFUL = 75	LESS = 55
OPTIC = 63	KOSHER = 76	EQUAL = 56
LOOK = 53	LOVING = 79	LOOK = 53
FRAME = 43	SELFISH = 78	EYES = 54
LAND CENTRE = 96	LORD = 49	LAWS = 55
COMPASS = 86	SHIVA = 59	LOVE = 54
LAST = 52	LOW = 50	LOVE FISH = 96
SHOT = 62	PRICE = 51	RED FISH = 69
LIGHTS= 75	LIQUOR = 92	LOVE = 54
ENERGY = 74	SPIRIT = 91	PATH = 45
LEGAL AID = 51	LIGHT = 56	LIGHT = 56
MEDICAL AID = 61	HEAVEN = 55	GLOW = 57
LIMITED = 72	LAND = 31	LIGHT = 56
MEASURE = 82	MINE = 41	GLOWED = 66
LIMITED = 72	LEONARDO DA VINCI = 146	LIGHT QUANTA = 130
LIMITS = 82	HEAVENLY BODIES = 146	WEST AND EAST = 131
LOG = 34	LOGIC = 46	LIVE = 48
EYE = 35	ETHICS = 64	SEX = 48
LUKE = 49	LOGIC = 46	LAND = 31
PAUL = 50	LOGO = 49	MINE = 41
LSD = 35	LANGUAGE = 68	LABOUR = 69
TAO = 36	SIGNS = 68	FATIGUE = 69
LAWYER = 84	LEGS = 43	LIT = 41
JURY = 74	ARSE = 43	BOX = 41
LOUD = 52	LIFE = 32	LAND MARK = 74
NOISE = 62	BITCH = 42	THE BEACON = 73
LOUD = 52	LAST = 52	LOUD = 52
SHOT = 62	DOLLAR = 62	REAR = 42
LIFE = 32	LOOKED = 62	LOIS = 55
ECHO = 31	FIRST = 72	CLARK = 45
LEGS = 43	LOOKED = 62	LABOUR = 69
TAIL = 42	ORIGIN = 72	COURTS = 96
LUCIFER = 74	LIFE = 32	LEGAL MIND = 77
HELL-FIRE = 75	MAGIC = 33	LEGAL LIAR = 77
LAZY = 64	LOVE = 54	LIES = 45
DONKEY = 74	PLAY = 54	OATH = 44
LONG = 48	LIFE = 32	LEGAL OATH = 81
TIME = 47	GIFT = 42	LEGAL LIES = 82
LEGAL = 37	LADY = 42	LEGAL LIARS = 96
JUDGE = 47	SHIP = 52	LEGAL MINDS = 96
LEGAL = 37	LONDON = 74	LETTER = 80
LAW = 36	ENGLISH = 74	POST = 70
LESS = 55	LARVAE = 59	LETTER = 80
EQUAL = 56	PUPAE = 59	WORDS = 79
LOOT = 62	LEVEL = 56	LOUD = 52
MONEY = 72	LEVEL'ED = 65	NOISE = 62

LOUD = 52
ROAR = 52

LASER = 55
LIGHT = 56

LEARNS = 69
MOTHER = 79

LEARNS = 69
TEACHERS = 79

LOSS = 65
LOST = 66

LATEST = 77
RATINGS = 88

LIBERAL = 59
LIARS = 59

LUCKS = 66
LIPS = 56

LUCKY = 72
LOTTO = 82

LUCKY = 72
NUMBER = 73

LAID = 26
REST = 62

LATE = 38
NITE = 48

LATIN = 56
ALPHABET = 65

LASER = 55
GAMES = 45

LORD = 49
ANGEL = 39

LEFT = 43
WING = 53

LOOK = 53
LEFT = 43

LABOUR = 69
FOR HIRE = 79

LOG = 34
BOOK = 43

LAUGHING = 79
NATURE = 79

LIARS = 59
STOPPED = 95

LILET = 58
BLOOD = 48

LETHAL = 58
BLOOD = 48

LETHAL = 58
BALANCE = 38

LIBERTY LIFE = 123
LEGISLATION = 123

LUMINARY = 113
CHRIST IMAGE = 112

LUMINARY = 113
COMPENDIUM = 113

LIFT OFF = 74
TAKE OFF = 64

LAST = 52
ACTION = 62

LAST = 52
QUEEN = 62

LONGEVITY = 129
HOLLYWOOD = 129

LINGUA = 64
FRANCA = 43

M

MANAS = 48
MONAD = 47

MOTHER = 79
HUSBAND =69

MOTHER = 79
MID-WIFE = 69

MODES = 56
BODY = 46

MA = 14
MOM = 41

MOON = 57
STAR = 58

MIND = 40
KEY = 41

MY = 38
SON = 48

MY = 38
ANGEL = 39

MY = 38
DEAR = 28

MESSAGE = 69
WORDS = 79

MAGNETIC = 72
DANCE = 27

MEN = 32
WAR = 42

MAGNETIC = 72

COUNT = 73

MEIN = 41
KAMP = 41

MIND = 40
DREAM = 41

MAFIA = 30
MOB = 30

MADNESS = 75
BRAIN DAMAGE = 75

MADNESS = 75
PARANOIA = 75

MADNESS = 75
DOCTOR = 75

METAL = 51
STEEL = 61

MOON = 57
LIGHT = 56

MOON = 57
TIME = 47

MACHINE = 53
PLANT = 63

MACHINE = 53
RUN = 53

MEASURE = 82
WEIGHT = 72

MAN = 28
KIND = 38

MAGIC = 33
LIFE = 32

MOTION = 86
INERTIA = 76

MEANS = 52
ENDS = 42

MASTER'S = 95
ARCHIVES = 85

MARS = 51
THOR = 61

MARCH = 43
WAR = 42

MIND KEY = 81
I THINK = 71

MIND KEY = 81
TEMPLE = 71

MIND LOCK = 81
I DOUBT = 71

MIND = 40

MINE = 41

MOON = 57
WALK = 47

MONAD = 47
OLOGY = 74

MEDICINE = 62
MUTI = 63

MEDICINE = 62
PLANT = 63

MUTI = 63
PLANT = 63

MEDICINES = 81
GENETICS = 82

MAIDEN = 46
GIRL = 46

MAIDEN = 46
FRIEND = 56

MOON = 57
WATER = 67

MOON = 57
LEVEL = 56

MILK = 45
CHEESE = 45

MEASURE = 82
WORLD = 72

MAGNETIC = 72
CODE = 27

MONARCHY = 97
SOCIETY = 96

MAN = 28
BOAT = 38

MONKEY = 83
PRIMATE = 82

MONKEY = 83
TUTU = 82

MIND OFGOD = 87
KEY OF GOD = 87

MESSAIH = 74
JESUS = 74

MESSAIH = 74
LUCIFER = 74

MADNESS = 75
MESSIAH = 74

MONAD = 47
POINT = 74

MONEY = 72

COUNT = 73

MAGNETIC = 72
MONEY = 72

MAGNETIC = 72
WORLD = 72

MAGNETIC = 72
ORIGIN = 72

MADNESS = 75
SPLIT = 76

MODUS = 72
OPERANDI = 82

MICRO = 58
SCOPE = 58

MIND KEY = 81
THINKS = 81

MALTESE = 75
CROSS = 74

MINUTE = 82
HOURS = 81

MARS = 51
NATO = 50

MARS = 51
AMERICA = 50

MOUNT = 83
OLIVES = 82

MUTABLE = 74
ENERGY = 74

MORAL = 59
ORDER = 60

MERIDIAN = 73
RADIUS = 72

MENTAL = 65
STATE = 65

MERCY = 64
JESUS = 74

MAGNETIC = 72
NUMBER = 73

MAGNETIC = 72
COUNT = 73

MENTAL = 65
MADNESS = 75

MOUNT = 83
OLIVES = 82

MONADS = 66
MATTER = 77

MATTER = 77

THE GOD HEAD = 77

CHRIST = 77
MATTER = 77

MATTER = 77
ADAM KADMON = 77

MAGNETIC CURRENT = 171
THE ELECTRIC TRAIN = 170

MAGNETIC CURRENT SQUARED = 256
THE HOLY ALPHABET OF CHRIST = 256

MAGNETIC CURRENT SQUARED = 256
THE MASTER OF SYMBOLISM = 257

MAGNETIC CURRENT SQUARED = 256
THE KNOWLEDGE OF SYMBOLS = 255

MEDIAN = 46
NERVE = 64

MIDDLE = 47
PLACE = 37

MASTER = 76
GURU = 67

LAY = 38
MAN = 28

MASTERS = 95
CAN BE FOUND = 85

MUSICAL = 78
WORDS = 79

MUSICAL = 78
HYMNS = 79

MILD = 38
WILD = 48

MOTHER = 79
WHORE = 69

MUSIC = 65
SONG = 55

MAGNITUDE = 94
DISTANCES = 94

MONEY = 72
DRIVEN = 72

MATTER = 77
ABSORBS = 76

MATTER = 77
WATER = 76

MAGNETIC = 72
IMPACT = 62

MASS = 52
FORM = 52

MARIE = 46
CURIE = 56

MODERN = 69
ECONOMICS = 96

MAKULA = 59
COOLIE = 59

MINDED = 49
MINDS = 59

MINE = 41
MIND = 40

MATERIAL = 79
WEALTH = 69

MATERIAL = 79
MAGNETS = 79

MISFITS = 95
SOCIETY = 96

THE MAFIA MOB = 93
NEWS MEDIA = 93

MAFIA = 30
FILM = 40

MEDICAL FILE = 79
LEGAL FILE = 69

MERMAID = 63
MERMAN = 64

MIND = 40
OPEN = 50

MERCY = 64
DIVINE = 63

MOEDER = 60
KINDER = 61

MANDRAX = 75
WHITE = 65

MASTER PIECE = 114
MASTER BALANCE = 114

MATRIX = 85
THE WOMB = 86

MASTER = 76
GURU = 67

MANDELAS = 69
SEA GULLS = 96

MOVIE STAR = 122
SHADOW OF LIFE = 123

MIDWAY = 75
DIAMETER = 75

MIDWAY = 75
DISTANCE = 75

MAGNETIC = 72
COUNT = 73

MOUNT = 83
HORSES = 84

MADAM = 32
EVE = 32

MAKE HAY = 64
SUN = 54

MAYOR = 72
TOWN = 72

MOA-ISM = 70
THE LAW = 69

MASTER'S = 95
KNOWLEDGE = 96

MASTER'S = 95
SOCIETY = 96

MELODIST = 97
MELODY LEAD = 96

MIRAGE = 53
BLUR = 53

MIRAGE = 53
IMAGE = 35

MAJOR = 57
CHANGES = 57

MAGNETIC FISH = 114
SIX AND NINE = 113

MAGNETIC FISH = 114
YING AND YANG = 114

MAGNETIC = 72
NUMBER = 73

MOVIE = 64
ENERGY = 74

MOVIE STAR = 122
SECOND COMING = 121

MOVIE STAR = 122
REVELATION = 121

MOVIE STAR = 122
PROPHESY = 122

MOVIE = 64
BEAUTY = 74

MEDIAN = 46
MIDDLE = 47

MEMORY = 89
REMEMBER = 79

MEMORY = 89
THE PAST = 89

MARS = 51
LANDING = 61

MASTER = 76
CONTROL = 97

MARGARET = 83
THATCHER = 83

MAMA = 28
AFRICA = 38

MANDELA'S = 69
COMRADE = 59

MEMORISE = 97
KNOWLEDGE = 96

MEMORY = 89
FORGETS = 90

MAGNETS = 79
MIND SEE = 69

MADELA'S = 69
YEARS = 68

MIRROR-IMAGE = 126
HOLLYWOOD = 129

MAGNETIC = 72
STRIP = 82

MARATHON = 90
RUNNER = 90

MICRO = 58
CITY = 57

MOTHER = 79
GRUNDY = 89

MOEDERS = 79
VADERS = 69
MOLAR = 59
TEETH = 58

MOUSE = 73
HUNT = 63

MANGLED = 56
MESS = 56

N

NEPTUNE = 95
TRITON = 96

NUMBERS = 92
NUMBERED = 82

NEW = 42
LIFE = 32

NEXT = 63

SHOT = 62

NIRVANA = 79
KRISHNA = 80

NIRVANA = 79
NATURE = 79

NORWAY = 96
SCANDINAVIA = 97

NEGATIVE = 83
NUMBER = 73

NUMBER = 73
TALKING = 74

NUMBER = 73
RATIO = 63

NAVIGATE = 79
THE PATH = 78

NAVIGATOR = 107
THE CROSS = 107

NUMBERS = 92
MEASURE = 82

NUMEROLOGY = 145
NATURAL SCIENCE = 145

NAVIGATE = 79
MAGNETS = 79

NATURAL LIGHT = 143
CROSS OF TIME = 142

NEEDS = 47
BUY = 48

NULL = 59
AND VOID = 69

NEW = 42
HOME = 41

NUCLEAR = 74
FUSION = 84

NUCLEAR = 74
ENERGY = 74

NATURE = 79
STUDY = 89

NARROW = 89
VISION = 88

NAZI = 50
AMERICA = 50

NAZ' ISM = 82
HITLER = 72

NAZ' ISM = 82
APARTHEID = 82

NAZ'ISM = 82

ORIGIN = 72

NAIL = 36
BITE = 36

NEW = 42
BOY = 42

BOY = 42
BLOCK = 43

BITCH = 42
BLOCK = 43

NEW = 42
KIDS = 43

NICKEL = 54
COBALT = 53

NEWS = 61
EDITOR = 71

NEWS = 61
ROOM = 61

NEW = 42
HOME = 41

NEWS EDITOR = 132
NEWS ROOM = 122

NEW = 42
DAWN = 42

NUTS = 74
MADNESS = 75

NEPTUNE = 95
TRITON = 96

NUCLEAR = 74
TEST = 64

NUCLEAR = 74
DIS-CHARGE = 74

NECK = 33
TIE = 34

NURSES = 96
MID-WIFE = 69

NO WAY = 49
HOSEA = 48

NAZIS = 69
MUNICH = 68

NAZIS = 69
THE AWB = 59

NEWS = 61
CODEX = 51

NEWS = 61
EDITOR = 71

NEW = 42

DAWN = 42

NEWS EDITOR = 132
NEWS ROOM = 122

NUTS = 74
MADNESS = 75

NATURAL ORDER = 147
DIVINE ENERGY   = 137

NATURAL ORDER = 147
NUCLEAR DISCHARGE = 148

NURSES = 96
BED PATIENT = 96

NEIGHBOUR = 99
SERVANT   = 99

NIGHT = 58
READING = 58

NITE = 48
CLUB = 38

NEW = 42
ACT = 24

NAZIS = 69
MUNICH = 68

NAZIS = 69
THE A. W. B. = 59

NATURAL = 87
SCIENCES = 77

NATURAL = 87
JUSTICE   = 87

NUMEROLOGIST = 168
DARRELL GONTIER = 158

NUNS = 68
BROTHER = 86

NUNS = 68
PENGUIN = 86

NATURAL = 87
SELECTOR = 97

NATURAL SELECTION = 189
SYNOPTIC LANGUAGE = 189

NOT = 49
SOLD = 50

NOW = 52
AND AGAIN = 51

NEO CORTEX = 119
SCIENCE OF MIND = 119

NERVE = 64
CENTRE = 65

O

OLD = 31
AGE = 13

OLD = 31
SAGE = 32

OLD = 31
LIFE = 32

OLD = 31
MEN = 32

ORAL = 46
LAW = 36

ODOUR = 73
ARSE HOLE = 83

O.T. = 35
N.T. = 34

O.T.& N.T = 69
ANCIENT BIBLE = 96

O.T./N. T. = 69
LABOUR = 69

OFFER = 50
WAVE = 51

ONE = 34
EYE = 35

ONE-EYE = 69
PIRATE = 69

ONE-EYE = 69
BLIND-MAN = 69

ONE = 34
ALLAH = 34

ONE = 34
BINAH = 34

ONE = 34
FREE = 34

ONE = 34
IMAGE = 35

ALLAH = 34
IMAGE = 35

NAKED = 35
ONE = 34

NAKED = 35
CAMEL = 34

OUT = 56
PUT = 57

OIL = 36
FIELD = 36

OUT-SIDE = 93
WITHIN = 83

ONIONS = 86
POTATO = 87

OPENED = 59
CLOSED = 58

OVUM = 71
SPERM = 71

OUT = 56
CRY = 46

OMEN = 47
MOON = 57

OMEN = 47
TIME = 47

OMEN = 47
DOOM = 47

OMEN = 47
THE DEAD = 47

OMEN = 47
BEAST = 47

ORIGIN = 72
SIDE REAL = 73

ORGASM = 73
A SPERM = 72

ORGASM = 73
THE FUCK = 74

ORIGIN = 72
SPERM = 71

ORGANISM = 96
THE COME = 69

ORGANISM = 96
DIVINE SEED = 96

ORGANISM = 96
THE PLANT = 96

ORE = 28
GOLD = 38

ON = 29
HOLD = 39

ON-HOLD = 68
ON-LINE = 69

OSCILLATION = 129
VIBRATIONS = 129

OSCILLATION = 129
SIXTY - NINE = 139

OSCILLATION = 129
NINETY - SIX = 139

OSCILLATION = 129
GONTIERISM = 129

OVER = 60
VIEW = 59

OSCILLATION = 129
THE TIME CYCLE = 128

OVER-COME = 96
OUT OF IDEA = 96

OEDIPUS = 89
COMPLEX = 88

OEDIPUS = 89
MOTHER = 79

OCULAR = 70
CIRCLES = 69

ONE WORLD = 106
FREE WORLD = 106

ORGAN = 55
DONOR = 66

ONE UNDER = 96
THE COVER = 96

ODOUR = 73
FRAGRANCE = 73

ODOUR = 73
PERFUME = 74

OSCILLATING = 121
BI-DIRECTIONAL = 121

ONE = 34
FREE = 34

ONE = 34
CHANCE = 34

ORGASMIC = 85
THE EARTH = 85

ORGASMIC = 85
PYRAMID = 86

OUT OF = 77
MATTER = 77

OUT OF = 77
NOTHING = 87

OUT OF = 77
GENESIS = 78

ORBITAL = 77
WINDOW = 88

OUT = 56
COMES = 55

OWN = 52
PACE = 25

OUT = 56
THERE = 56

OLYMPIC = 93
LAUREATE = 83

OUT = 56
LAWS = 55

ORLANDO = 79
PIRATE = 69

ONE = 34
NIL = 35

ONE = 34
GOAL = 35

OXFORD = 82
SCHOOL = 72

OLD GUARD = 82
SCHOOL = 72

ON = 29
AIR = 28

OFF = 27
AIR = 28

OXFORD = 82
HARVARD = 72

OPEN = 50
HATCH = 40

P

PSYCHO-GENETIC = 149
GENETIC IN-BREEDING = 150

PI = 25
EARTH = 52

PI = 25
AREA = 25

PI-CIRCLE = 75
DIAMETER = 75

PI = 25
SFA = 25

PSYCHO-GENETIC = 149
THREE-SIX-NINE = 150

PIN = 39
HOLE = 40

POINT = 74
BLUFF = 47

PAY = 42
LOAD = 32

PAY = 42
SALT = 52

PEAS = 41
BEANS = 41

PUDDING = 75
TASTE   = 65

POOR = 64
WHITE = 65

PHOTO = 74
ELECTRIC = 75

PIK = 36
BOTHA = 46

POPULATION = 139
EXPLOSION = 129

PRICK = 57
PUSS = 75

PUSS = 75
IN BOOT = 75

PRICK = 57
CUNT   = 58

PRICK = 57
URINE = 67

PSYCHIC = 83
EYE OF GOD = 82

PART = 55
& PARCEL = 55

PUSS = 75
BOTTOM = 85

PATIENT = 85
DOCTOR = 75

PHILOSOPHY = 143
THE EMPIRIC LAW = 142

PARANOIA = 75
DOCTOR = 75

PARANOIA = 75
SIMPLE = 74

PAY-DAY = 72
MONEY = 72

PAY-DAY = 72
BONUS = 72

PAY-DAY = 72
DOLLAR = 62

PAY-DAY = 72
CROWN = 73

PRO- = 49
DUCT = 48

PRIMATE = 82
MAN = 28

PRIMATE = 83
MONKEY = 83

PRO- = 49
GRAM = 39

PRO- = 49
TINE = 48

PRO- = 49
PER = 39

PRO- = 49
JECT = 48

PARASITE = 89
VIRUS = 89

PORK = 60
SWINE = 70

PEARLS = 71
SWINE = 70

POLITICAL = 97
SOCIETY = 96

PULP = 65
PAPER = 56

PAPER = 56
MONDI = 55

POINT = 74
IN T IME = 47

PEACE = 30
OF MIND = 40

POLAR = 62
BEAR = 26

POLARISATION = 149
CHEMICAL REACTION = 139

POLICE = 60
BRASS = 59

POLICE DAD = 69
LE GRANGE = 69

PAY- = 42
MENT = 52

PIPE-LINE = 86
TUNNEL = 68

PAROLE = 67
PARDON = 68

PARALLEL-O-GRAM = 131
PYTHAGORAS = 130

PERFECT = 73
NUMBER = 73

PREFECT = 73
SCHOOL = 72

PERCEPTION = 121
THE VISION = 121

PSYCHIATRIST = 167
THE LOCK OF THE MIND = 168

PSYCHIATRY = 144
PSYCHOLOGY = 145

PARABLES = 74
DIALOGUE = 74

PARABLES = 74
PARANOIA = 75

PSYCHIATRIST = 167
THE RAPE OF THE MIND = 167

PIANO = 55
PLAY = 54

PIANO = 55
ORGAN = 55

PRESS = 77
FREEDOM = 66

PERFECT = 73
SCHOOL = 72

PROOF OF LIFE = 123
THE HOLY BIBLE = 123

PLAY = 54
SONG = 55

PARCH = 46
DRY = 47

PEA- = 22
COCK = 32

PARCHED = 55
SUN = 54

PEOPLE = 69
DYING = 59

PHOTON = 88
ELECTRICAL = 88

PARTICLE = 84
ENERGY = 74

PARTICLE OF LIGHT = 151
JESUS CHRIST = 151

PEOPLE = 69
RACIST = 59

PEOPLE = 69
ANIMALS = 69

PEOPLE = 69
DARWIN = 69

PEOPLE = 69
VEGETABLE = 79

PERPETUAL ENERGY = 188
H-TIMES FREQUENCY = 188

PERPETUAL ENERGY = 188
OPTICAL ILLUSION = 187

PERPETUAL ENERGY = 188
THE BEGINNING AND THE END = 189

PHOTO = 74
COLOUR = 84

PHOTON = 88
BLACK AND BLUE = 88

PURSE = 79
WEALTH = 69

PARTICLE THEORY = 175
ELECTRIC CURRENT = 174

PARTICLE THEORY = 175
ELECTRIC THOUGHT = 174

PROPHESY = 122
REVELATION = 121

PRIMITIVE = 121
SOUTH AFRICA = 121

PARTICLE = 84
TERRAIN = 85

PLEASURE = 97
RESERVED = 96

PLEASURE = 97
GAURANTEED = 96

PRINCE = 65
CHARLES = 66

PRINCE = 65
ANDREW = 65

POOR = 64
BRAHMIN = 65

PENIS = 63
OBELISK = 73

PAPACY = 62
POPE = 52

PAPACY = 62
CARDINAL = 62

PAPACY = 62
QUEEN = 62

PUSS = 75
SNOOK = 74

PUNCTUAL = 108
ANNO DOMINI = 108

PENIS = 63
SNOEK = 64

PEOPLE'S = 88

COURT = 77

POLICE = 60
KEEPER = 60

PURE = 60
NAZI = 50

PRO- = 49
FOR = 39

PHYSICAL SCIENCE = 151
GENETIC IN-BREEDING = 150

PEANUTS = 96
& POPCORN = 97

PHOTO-FINISH = 139
CHEMICAL REACTION = 139

PHOTO-FINISH = 139
HOLLYWOOD = 129

PANDORA'S BOX = 129
HOLLYWOOD =129

PANDORA'S KEY = 129
GONTIERISM = 129

PUT = 57
INTO = 58

PEANUTS = 96
UNSALTED = 96

PREDICTABLE = 95
HUMOUR = 96

PLATO = 64
GREEK = 46

PEARL OF = 73
WISDOM = 83

PACK = 31
AGE = 13

PAPA-RAZZI = 114
THIRD-EYES = 113

PUBLICITY = 117
NEWS-PAPER = 117

PONDER = 72
THINK = 62

PONDER = 72
'I THINK' = 71

PONDER = 72
DOUBT = 62

PILLAR = 68
PYRAMID = 86

PLASMA = 62
OVER-LOAD = 92

PHONE = 58

SKAKEL = 59

POPSICKLE = 106
SUCKERS = 96

Q

QUANTUM WAVE = 158
TWIST OF TIME = 159

QUANTUM WAVE = 158
NORTH & SOUTH = 158

QUANTUM LEAP = 141
RELATIVITY = 141

QUANTUM LEAP = 141
PURGATORY = 141

QUANTUM LEAP = 141
BOTTOMLESS = 140

QUANTUM FIELD = 143
MECHANICAL ENERGY = 143

QUANTUM FIELD = 143
ANTI-CLOCK WISE = 144

QUANTUM PHYSIC = 187
OPTICAL ILLUSION = 187

QUANTUM PHYSIC = 187
POTENTIAL ENERGY = 186

QUANTUM PHYSIC = 187
POTENTIAL UNCLEAR = 186

QUANTUM PHYSIC = 187
ELECTRO MAGNETIC FIELD = 186

QUEER = 66
DUAL-MAN = 66

QUEER = 66
WOMAN = 66

QUEER DRAG = 96
JUDGE'S -DRAG = 96

QUANTUM PHYSIC = 187
PERPETUAL ENERGY = 188

QUEER = 66
MANKIND = 66

QUERY = 86
KNOWLEDGE = 96

QUERY = 86
JUSTICE = 87

QUIET = 72
SOUND = 73

QUADRANT = 96
COMPASS = 86

QUICK = 61
REST = 62

QUICK = 61
PAUSE = 62

QUIZ = 73
SCHOOL = 72

QUOTE = 78
WORDS = 79

QUOTA = 74
NUMBER = 73

QUICKLY = 98
CURRENT = 99

QUANTUM MECHANICS = 182
YOT-HUH-WAW-HUH = 181

QUANTUM = 107
MATHEMATICAL = 106

QUANTUM = 107
THE POINT = 107

QUANTUM = 107
THE MESSIAH = 107

QUANTUM = 107
INTERIOR = 108

QUANTA = 74
ENERGY = 74

QUANTUM OF ENERGY = 202
TOTAL SOLAR ECLIPSE = 202

R

RISE = 51
MELT = 50

RICH = 38
MAN = 28

RIVER = 72
JORDAN = 62

ROCK = 47
& ROLL = 57

RED CROSS = 101
VIS-A-VIS = 101

RED CROSS = 101
SKELETON = 101

RED ROSE = 84
& CROSS = 74

ROMAN = 61
CATHOLIC = 71

ROMAN = 61
CHURCH = 61

ROME = 51
ROMAN = 61

ROMAN = 61
HOMO = 51

ROMAN = 61
PARISH = 71

ROMAN = 61
TEMPLE = 71

RAT = 39
HOLE = 40

RIPE = 48
GREEN = 49

RACE CAR = 49
ACCIDENT = 59

RACE CAR = 49
SPEED = 49

RACE CAR TIME = 96
SPEED TIME = 96

RAPE = 40
FUCK = 41

RUGBY = 73
SOCCER = 63

ROUND = 72
BALL = 27

ROUND = 72
WORLD = 72

RUGBY = 73
FOOT-BALL = 83

REASONABLE DOUBT = 154
MISSING LINGS = 155

REASONABLE = 92
THEORY = 91

REBIRTH = 80
BORN AGAIN = 81

RUSSIA = 87
MOSCOW = 88

RING = 48
of FIRE = 38

RING = 48
of DEATH = 38

REASON = 72
for DOUBT = 62

RESPECT = 86
of KNOWLEDGE = 96

RESPECT = 86
of SOCIETY = 96

RESCOGITANS = 130
THE MIDDLE WAY = 129

REAL = 36
HELL = 37

REAL LIFE = 68
LANGUAGE = 68

REAL = 36
BEING = 37

REAL-MAN = 64
HAS-BEING = 65

REAL-MAN = 64
HERO = 46

RATIONAL KNOWLEDGE = 186
LOOK AND LEARN METHOD = 187

RADIAL = 45
MEDIAN = 46

ROLLING = 87
MATTER = 77

ROLLS = 76
WATER = 67

RUN = 53
PLANT = 63

ROCK = 47
MIX = 46

ROCK = 47
BODY = 46

ROCK = 47
TIME = 47

ROCK = 47
MONAD = 47

RULES = 75
THE KING = 74

ROBES = 59
& GOWN = 59

ROBES = 59
& WIGS = 58

REVOLUTION = 151
QUANTUM LEAP = 141

REVOLUTION = 151
JESUS CHRIST = 151

RADIO ACTIVITY = 156
ASTRONOMERS = 157

RADIUM = 66
FISHES = 66

ROSE & CROSS = 131
ROSICRUCIAN = 130

ROSE AND CROSS = 150
ROSICRUCIANS = 149

ROMEO = 66
& JULIET = 77

ROAD = 38
SIDE = 37

RE- = 23
MAND = 32

RE- = 23
JAIL = 32

RURAL = 70
PEOPLE = 69

RAINBOW = 82
WORLD = 72

RACISM = 63
CYNICS = 73

REPUBLIC = 86
CITIZEN = 86

REPUBLIC = 86
SOCIETY = 96

REPUBLIC = 86
DENIZENS = 96

RE-SALE = 60
VALUE = 61

RAINBOW = 82
FOLLOW = 83

RAINBOW = 82
RECORDS = 82

RAINBOW = 82
LIFE-SPAN = 82

ROMANCE = 69
MARRIAGE-ACT = 96

ROMANCE = 69
MOM AND DAD = 69

ROMANCE = 69
LOVING = 79

ROMANCE = 69
PLAYBOY = 96

ROMANCE = 69
FAT-LADY = 69

RONALD = 64
REAGAN = 46

ROMAN = 61
CRUSADE = 71

ROLLER = 80
COASTER = 81

ROTE = 58
KORAN = 59

RED = 27
DOG = 26

RED-TAPE = 69
PUBLISHED = 96

REWARD = 69
PEANUTS = 96

REWARD = 69
DEAD OR ALIVE = 96

REWARD = 69
A WANTED MAN = 96

RESIDES = 79
INSIDE BEING = 97

ROOK = 59
CASTLE = 60

RE- = 23
ACT = 24

ROCK = 47
LEGEND = 47

ROCK = 47
THE KING = 74

ROCK = 47
& POP = 47

ROCK = 47
& SEX = 48

REFRESH = 79
WATER = 67

REPUTATION = 139
THE LAWS OF MIND = 149

REPUTATION = 139
CHRIST HIMSELF = 149

ROLL = 57
OUT = 56

RIO DA = 47
NATAL = 48

RIGHT = 62
STUFF = 72

ROTARY = 97
ROTARIAN = 96

ROTATES = 79
THE LAW = 69

ROSE = 57
OF ENGLAND = 57

ROLE = 50
MODEL = 49

RARELY = 79
FOUNDED = 69

REEBOK = 56
SHOES = 66

S

SPIRACULUM VITOE = 204
MANIFESTED OMNISCIENCE = 205

SOCCER = 63
FIELD = 36

SOUTH = 83
AFRICA = 38

SKY = 55
LIGHT = 56

SOUTH AFRICA = 121
AUSTRALIA = 120

STUCK = 74
IN TIME = 47

LOOK = 53
SEEN = 43

LOOK = 53
SAW = 43

SEA = 25
EARTH = 52

SEA-BED = 36
EARTH-BED = 63

SALT = 52
SEA = 25

SEVEN = 65
SEALS = 56

SON = 48
DAUGHTER = 84

SON = 48
FATHER = 58

SEA- = 25
GULL = 52

SEA = 25
SHIP = 52

SHADOW = 70
BOXING = 71

SHADOW = 70
GHOST = 69

SPIRAL = 75
POINT = 74

STONE = 73
CONCRETE = 83

SPECIAL DELIVERY = 165
ELECTRICAL POWER = 165

SPECIAL = 65

TACTICS = 75

SPECIAL = 65
TACTIC = 56

STATE = 65
OF ISRAEL = 64

SHIP- = 52
MENT = 52

SMITH = 69
APPLES = 69

SMOKING = 88
CIGARETTE = 88

SMOKING = 88
NICOTINE = 89

SMOKING = 88
MARIJUANA = 88

SOLUTION = 125
MYSTERY = 125

SOLUTION = 125
CONCLUSION = 125

SALTY = 77
WATER = 67

SAINT = 63
PETER = 64

SAINT = 63
JOSEPH = 73

SOLAR = 65
LUNAR = 66

SUN = 54
BURN = 55

STAR = 58
BIRTH = 57

STAR = 58
MOON = 57

STAR = 58
PLANET = 68

STAR = 58
THE EARTH = 85

STAR = 58
SCIENCE = 58

SURFACE = 73
ENERGY = 74

SKIES = 63
SURFACE = 73

SUN = 54
SET = 44

SUN = 54

PATH = 45

SUN = 54
EAST = 45

SIX = 52
NINE = 42

SIX = 52
FIVE = 42

SIXTY NINE = 139
NINETY SIX = 139

SHEEP = 53
GOAT = 43

SANAT = 55
KUMARA = 65

SURFACE = 73
LIMIT = 63

SIX = 52
TIES = 53

SAD = 24
SACK = 34

SAD SACK = 58
ARMY = 57

SHOW = 65
DOWN = 56

SEX = 48
STAR = 58

SEXY = 73
SLUT = 72

SENSES = 81
EYE OF GOD = 82

SHINES = 74
BRIGHT = 64

SHUT = 58
CLOSED = 68

SUGAR = 66
URINE = 67

SUGAR-MAN = 94
SUGAR-DADDY = 104

SUGAR-MAN = 94
UNICORN = 94

SPACE = 44
MARCH = 43

SHOT = 62
GUNS = 61

SCHOOL = 72
CHILDREN = 73

SUGAR = 66

HONEY = 67	THE DEAD = 47	YIN AND YANG = 114
STARCH = 69 DRUGS = 69	SLEEP = 57 WALK = 47	SEEING... = 59 'I BELIEVE' = 69
SECULAR = 79 RELIGION = 89	SLEEP = 57 WORK = 67	SOUL = 67 MATTER = 77
SECULAR = 79 TEXT = 69	SERIAL = 64 KILLING = 74	SOUL = 67 CHRIST = 77
SCAPE = 44 GOAT = 43	SABBATH DAY = 83 SUNDAY = 84	SOULS = 86 PYRAMID = 86
SELF = 42 GOING = 52	SWEET = 72 SOUR = 73	SOULS = 86 OF MANKIND = 87
SEX = 48 CHANGE = 38	SELF MEETS SELF = 146 PAST & FUTURE = 147	SELF = 42 DEFENCE = 42
SEX = 48 BALANCE = 38	SELF MEETS SELF = 146 FISH MEETS FISH = 146	SELF - EGO = 69 SELF LOVE = 96
SOCKS = 67 & SHOES = 66	SELF MEETS SELF = 146 THE YIN AND YANG = 147	SALIVA = 64 RABIES = 54
STOCK = 68 EXCHANGE = 67	SOUR = 73 BITTER = 74	SALLY = 69 & HARRY = 70
STOCK = 68 MARKET = 68	SUN-GOD = 80 BORN AGAIN = 81	SLAVE = 59 LABOUR = 69
STOCK = 68 WEALTH = 69	SUN-GOD = 80 KING-DAVID = 81	SLAVE = 59 COOLIE = 59
STOCK = 68 & STOCK = 68	STOP = 70 ROBOT = 70	SLAVE = 59 MAKULA = 59
SOLDIER = 82 MAN = 28	SCREW = 68 WARDER = 69	SLAVE = 59 LIARS = 59
SOLDIER = 82 MONKEY = 83	SCREW = 68 WHORE = 69	SPOOK = 76 GHOST = 69
SICK = 42 WELL = 52	SCREW = 68 FAT-BITCH = 69	SUN-GOD = 80 HOLY RA = 79
SACRED IMAGE = 85 STATUE = 86	SCREW = 68 FAT-BOY = 69	SPEED = 49 ACCIDENT = 59
STATUE = 86 PYRAMID = 86	STAR = 58 SIGNS = 68	SPOOKS = 95 SPOOKED = 85
STATUE = 86 SACRED EYE = 85	SON = 48 TROOP = 84	SHARK = 57 ATTACK = 56
STATUE = 86 BUSH LAW = 86	SON = 48 DAUGHTER = 84	SCREAM = 59 GHOST = 69
STATUE = 86 JUDICIAL CODE = 96	SIDE = 37 REAL = 36	SAVE = 47 KEEP = 37
SLEEP = 57 NIGHT = 58	SCORN = 69 FURY = 70	SLAVE = 59 SERVE = 69
SLEEP = 57 TIME = 47	SECOND = 60 COMING = 61	SERVE = 69 SOCIETY = 96
SLEEP = 57	SIX AND NINE = 113	SERVE = 69

PEOPLE = 69	STAND = 58	CITY = 57
SERVE = 69 THE PUBLIC = 96	SCREEN = 64 HERO = 46	SKI- = 39 BOAT = 38
SERVE = 69 BETTER = 70	SCREEN = 64 TEST = 64	SIGN = 49 OF JONAH = 48
STAR -LIGHT = 114 MOON-LIGHT = 113	SITS = 67 & STANDS = 77	SPARKS = 84 ENERGY = 74
SAVING = 72 MONEY = 72	SITTING = 98 & STANDING = 88	SOLAR SYSTEM = 166 NUCLEAR FISSION = 165
SAVING = 72 DOLLAR = 62	SCOT = 57 WELSH = 67	SOLAR SYSTEM = 166 THE TRIPLE SIX = 165
SET = 44 FREE = 34	SCOTCH = 68 WELCH = 67	SIDE = 37 ROAD = 38
SAINT PETER = 127 SAINT LUCIFER = 137	SEE = 29 READ = 28	SALT = 52 EARTH = 52
SILENT MOVIE = 143 SOUND OF FILM = 134	SAME = 28 BALANCE = 38	STELLA = 69 AURORAE = 79
SEX = 48 SHOP = 58	SAME = 38 ALIKE = 38	SPONGE = 76 WATER = 67
SHOP = 58 & BUY = 48	SHELL = 56 SHOCK = 56	SCHOOL = 72 BACK-WARDS = 82
SELL = 48 & BUY = 48	SHELL = 56 SHOCKED = 65	SPONGE = 76 ABSORBS = 76
SELL = 48 & SHOP = 58	STAKE = 56 OUT = 56	SOUND = 73 ENERGY = 74
SEX = 48 TRADE = 48	SOCIAL = 59 PEOPLE = 69	SOUNDS = 92 ELECTRON = 92
SHOP = 58 TRADE = 48	SOCIAL = 59 SCIENCE = 58	SOUND = 73 OF VOICES = 73
SEEING = 59 DOUBLE = 59	SUR- = 58 PLUS = 68	SOUND = 73 MOVIES = 83
SEEING = 59 COPY = 59	SUFFIX = 85 A PARTICLE = 85	SIMPLICITY = 135 THE FACTS OF LIFE = 135
SMOKE = 63 SCREEN = 64	SOCIETY = 96 CONTROL = 97	SANTA = 55 CLAUS = 56
SURF = 64 RAVE = 46	SOCIETY = 96 WATCHERS = 97	SAINT = 63 NICOLAS = 73
SURF = 64 ENERGY = 74	STOPPED = 95 KNOWLEDGE = 96	SIMPLE = 74 PARANOIA = 75
SURF-CELL = 96 SET FORM = 96	SMOKING = 88 CHIMNEY = 77	SAFE = 31 HOME = 41
SICK = 42 COW = 41	STAR-VATION = 139 TOP-SPORT = 139	SCREAMING = 89 MURDER = 79
SAI = 29 OM = 28	SNAPS = 69 & CLIPS = 59	SAFE = 31 JAIL = 32
SIT = 48	SPIN = 58	SAFE = 31

CASH = 31

SAFE = 31
KEY = 41

SEA-GULLS = 96
MANDELAS = 69

SCRIPT = 85
WRITE = 75

SKY = 55
DANCER = 45

STOOD = 73
STILL = 72

SCREEN = 64
PLAY = 54

SNOOKER = 97
CHAMPION = 79

SPECIAL = 65
EFFECTS = 64

SPECIAL-EFFECTS = 129
HOLLYWOOD = 129

SAKIE = 45
DE KOK = 46

SWEET = 72
LEKKER = 62

SPEECH = 56
SPOKE = 66

SPOKE = 66
OUT = 56

SPOKE = 66
WOMAN = 66

SUFFER = 75
CROSS = 74

SACRIFICE = 73
CROSS = 74

SACRIFICE = 73
JESUS = 74

SUFFERED = 84
MESSIAH = 74

SPIRAL = 75
CROSS = 74

SICKEL = 59
STAR = 58

STAR & SICKEL = 117
NEWSPAPER = 117

SICKEL = 59
HAMMER = 58

SAND = 38

MAN = 28

SOAP = 51
BOX = 41

SPRING-BOK = 111
ILLUSION = 111

SMOKE = 63
SIGNAL = 62

SEDATED = 58
SLEEP = 57

SMOKE = 63
DUST= 64

SERIEL = 68
KILLER = 67

STATUTE-BOOK = 149
A SCALE OF JUSTICE = 149

SAME = 38
PIECE = 38

SAME = 38
PLACE = 37

SLIVER = 85
OF GLASS = 58

SLOW = 69
STOP = 70

SLOW   = 69
FASTER = 69

SLOW = 69
TOO FAST = 96

SYMBOL = 86
OF JUSTICE = 87

SYMBOL = 86
OF NOTHING = 87

STONE-AGE = 86
PYRAMID = 86

STONE-AGE = 86
BROTHER = 86

STONE-AGE = 86
FREEMASON = 96

SANGOMAS = 89
NATURE = 79

SANGOMAS = 89
PROPHET = 98

SOUTH & NORTH = 158
STATE OF THE ART = 158

SOUTH & NORTH = 158
THREE DIMENSION = 158

SOUTH & NORTH = 158

FIELD OF MAGNETISM = 158

SOUTH & NORTH = 158
BONE OF SKELETON = 158

SET TO... = 79
CONTROL = 97

SWEAT = 68
SHOP = 58

STAMP = 69
GROUND = 79

STAMP = 69
WITH FEET = 96

STAMP = 69
THE FEET = 69

SALT = 52
FISH = 42

SUB- = 42
URB = 41

STEERING = 97
CONTROL = 97

SALT = 52
SPICE = 52

SPICE = 52
EARTH = 52

SPICE = 52
MEDICINE = 62

SEGREGATION = 120
SOUTH AFRICA = 121

SOUTH = 83
AFRICA = 38

SOUTH AFRICA = 121
REVELATION = 121

SHOUT = 83
SOUND = 73

STORY = 97
TELLING = 79

SMASHED = 69
MACHINERY = 96

SELLING = 78
NOTHING = 87

T

TELEGRAM = 81
LETTER = 80

TAPES = 61
& DISKS = 62

TEXT = 69
MESSAGE = 69

TEXT = 69
ANCIENT BIBLE = 96

TEXT CODE = 96
O.T. - N.T. = 69

TEXT-HAND = 96
JEHOVAH = 69

TEXT = 69
WORDS = 79

TEXT = 69
NUMERICAL = 96

TRI- = 47
ANGULAR = 74

TOTAL = 68
ECLIPSE = 69

TRAN- = 53
SHIP = 52

TRAIN = 62
SHIP = 52

THE ANCIENT LAW = 135
COMMANDMENTS = 134

THE ANCIENT BONE = 135
THE SKELETON = 134

TOOTH = 78
BRUSH = 68

TIME = 47
CYCLE = 48

THERMO = 79
DYNAMIC = 69

TRUE = 64
LOVE = 54

THE = 33
END = 23

THUNDER = 90
LIGHTNING = 100

THE BUDDHA = 73
THE MIND = 73

TUG = 48
BOAT = 38

TAKE = 37
CARE = 27

TAKE = 37
TIME = 47

TAKE = 37
COUNT = 73

TIME = 47
WALK = 47

TIME = 47
CRAWL = 57

THE GOVERNMENT = 166
THE THREE SIXES = 165

THE GOVERNMENT = 166
DISINFORMATION = 166

THE GOVERNMENT = 166
VICARIUS FILII DEI = 165

TWO = 58
ARE ONE = 58

THE TABLOID = 96
BULLETIN = 95

THE TABLOID = 96
RED-TAPE = 69

THE TABLOID = 96
PUBLISHED = 96

TRAIN = 62
TRIP = 63

THE 'I CHING' = 83
A LAW OF GOD = 84

THE 'I CHING' = 83
GOD FATHER = 84

THE 'I CHING' = 83
DOWISM = 83

THE 'I CHING' = 83
GENETICS = 82

THE 'I CHING' = 83
PSYCHIC = 83

THE CIRCLE = 83
THE SACRED = 83

THE CIRCLE = 83
A IMAGE OF GOD = 83

THE EARTH = 85
THE GRAVE = 86

THE GRAVE = 86
PYRAMID = 86

THE GRAVE = 86
VOODOO = 86

THE GRAVE = 86
SATANISM = 96

TOP = 51
ROOM = 61

TOP = 51
FULL = 51

TOP = 51
HEAVY = 61

TOP = 51
NEWS = 61

TODAY = 65
PAST = 56

THE 'I CHING' = 83
GOD SCIENCE = 84

TAKES = 56
GIVEN = 57

TABLE = 40
CHAIR = 39

THE CHILD = 69
MOM AND DAD = 69

TUNNEL = 86
PASSAGE = 68

THE MOUTH OF MYSTERY = 256
THE MASTER OF SYMBOLISM = 257

THE MASTER OF SYMBOLISM = 257
LIFE SUPPORT SYSTEM = 258

TWO = 58
SQUARED = 85

TRANSMIT = 114
SIX AND NINE = 113

THE WAY TO THE END = 173
WHAT A WAY TO HELL = 174

THE TAO = 69
THE LAW = 69

THE S.A.P. = 69
THE S.O.B. = 69

THE LAW = 69
JUDICIAL = 69

THE LAW = 69
COURTS = 96

THE LAW = 69
SOCIETY = 69

THE LAW = 69
LIARS = 59

THE TAO = 69
QIGONG = 69

THE TAO = 69
THE CHINESE = 96

THE TAO = 69
IS BINDING = 59

THEY = 58
CAN LEARN = 68

THE KNOWLEDGE OF A CHILD = 187
LOOK AND LEARN METHOD = 187

THE KNOWLEDGE OF SYMBOLS = 255
THE 'CHRIST' OF MYSTERY = 256

TEAM = 39
MATE = 39

THE TIME = 80
HOURS = 81

THE BEAST = 80
FOREHEADS = 81

THE BEAST = 80
THE MONAD = 80

THE BEAST = 80
THE OMEN = 80

TIME = 47
CURE = 47

THE WANDERING JEW = 166
THE GOVERNMENT = 166

THE WANDERING JEW = 166
THE TRIPLE SIX = 165

THINK = 62
FIRST = 72

THE DEAD OF = 60
NIGHT = 58

THIEF = 48
NIGHT = 58

TWIN RACE = 93
BLACK & WHITE = 94

TWIN RACE = 93
A COLOURED = 94

TOTEM = 73
CROSS = 74

THE LION = 83
FIRE = 38

TINA & IKE = 69
TURNER = 96

TIME-CODE = 74
TIME RACE = 74

THE DEAD CODE = 74
THE OMEGA = 74

TIME = 47
CROSS = 74

TIME = 47
PLACE = 37

THE DEAD = 47
HELL = 37

TIME ZONE = 107
THE CROSS = 107

TIME = 47
BEGIN = 37

THE CRUCIFIED = 111
CHRIST IMAGE = 112

THE CRUCIFIED = 111
THE GENESIS = 111

THE CRUCIFIED = 111
ADAM KADMON'S FACE = 111

THE CRUCIFIED = 111
THE GOD-HEAD'S FACE = 111

THE HOLY BIBLE = 123
ANCIENT EVIDENCE = 133

THE HOLY BIBLE = 123
TRIBUNE GOD-HEAD = 133

THE BIBLE WORD = 123
GOD'S VISION = 133

THE HOLY KEY = 134
COMMANDMENTS = 134

THE TREE OF LIFE = 134
THE SEX OF EVE = 134

THE BLOOD OF LIFE = 134
THE SKELETON = 134

THE SKELETON = 134
INFORMATION = 134

TECHNOLOGY = 124
INFORMATION = 134

TECHNOLOGICAL INFORMATION = 258
LIFE SUPPORT SYSTEM = 258

TECHNOLOGICAL INFORMATION = 258
THE CRUCIFIXION OF JESUS = 259

THE = 33
LIFE = 32

THE = 33
AGENDA = 32

TIME = 47
FAST = 46

THE A.N.C. = 51
ROME = 51

THE C.N.A. = 51
NEWS = 61

THE A.N.C. HEAD = 69
MANDELAS' = 69

THE A.N.C = 51

AFRICAN = 52

THE A.N.C = 51
MANDELA = 50

THE C.N.A. = 51
AMERICA = 50

THE C.N.A. = 51
NATO = 50

TIME = 47
STUCK = 74

TAIL = 42
LEGS = 43

TOMORROW = 137
PAST & FUTURE = 147

THE GOD-HEAD NAME = 110
THE CHRIST = 110

THE GOD-HEAD = 77
MAN-KIND = 66

THE LIGHT = 89
AND SHADOW = 89

THE PUBLIC = 96
CITIZEN = 86

THE OMEN = 80
MIND-KEY = 81

THE SACRED LAWS = 138
SELF KNOWLEDGE = 138

THE CHILD = 69
WELFARE = 70

THE RECORD = 96
WELFARE DATA = 96

THE KEY OF THE BIBLE = 158
THE ROMAN ALPHABET = 159

THE ROMAN ALPHABET = 159
WORD FOR WORD = 159

THE ROMAN ALPHABET = 159
THE WORDS OF GOD = 159

TEACH = 37
CHILDREN = 73

TEACH LIFE = 69
FROM BRAIN = 96

THE KING = 74
THE CHIEF = 64

TEA = 26
PEE = 26

TRI-   = 47
BUTE = 48

TAX = 45

CUT = 44

ALPHA-BRAVO = 96

IS HELL = 37

TAXES = 69
WEALTH = 69

THE CHURCH = 94
CONVENT = 93

TIME = 47
BEGIN = 37

TALIBAN = 59
KORAN = 59

THE SONG = 88
THE MUSIC = 98

TIME = 47
UP = 37

THE LAW = 69
KORAN = 59

THE SHADE = 70
SHADOW = 70

TAKE = 37
CARE = 27

THE LIGHT = 89
POLAROID = 90

TIME AND SPACE = 110
OMNI-SCIENCE = 109

TIME WARP = 105
PYRAMIDS = 105

THE ALPHA AND OMEGA = 131
DEVELOPMENT = 131

TIME AND SPACE = 110
TIME TRAX = 110

TIME WARP = 105
THE WORLD = 105

THE ALPHA AND OMEGA = 131
REVELATION = 121

TIME CODE = 74
ZERO = 64

TAKE = 37
A BREAK = 38

THE ACHES = 69
& PAINS = 59

MAGNET = 60
TECHNIK = 70

TAKE = 37
PLACE = 37

THE X-RAY = 101
SKELETON = 101

TREE OF = 69
KNOWLEDGE = 96

THE GENETIC CODE = 123
NUMERICAL CODE = 123

TALKING = 74
MOVIE = 64

THE SMOKE = 96
OF KNOWLEDGE = 96

THE HOLY BIBLE = 123
NUMERICAL CODE = 123

THE PROOF OF LIFE = 156
FISHERMEN'S KEY = 157

THE COVER = 96
COSTUME = 96

TAX = 45
LAWS = 55

THE CIRCLE = 83
BIO-ANARCHIC = 83

THE COVER = 96
UNIFORM = 96

TIME = 47
ALONE = 47

THINK = 62
SPEAK = 52

THE COVER = 96
THE BOOKS = 95

TEN = 39
PIN = 39

THOUGHT = 99
STUDY = 89

TRAN = 53
SPEC = 43

TAP = 37
DANCE = 27

TRUTH = 87
HURTS = 86

SPECIAL DELIVERY = 165
MESSAGE...FROM SPACE = 165

TURN = 73
ROUND = 72

THE S.A.P. = 69
ASKARI = 59

TROOPS = 103
MOUNTS = 102

TRAIN = 62
CARRIAGE = 62

THE RECORD = 96
THE S.A.P. = 69

THE ASIANS = 96
CIVIL WAR = 97

TELKOM S.A. = 96
CALL-BOX = 69

THE S.A.P. = 69
ROBBERS = 79

TEACHERS = 79
GHOST = 69

TREK = 54
SEARCH = 54

S.A.P.S. = 88
POLICEMAN = 88

THE LAW = 69
RACISM NAME = 96

THE STATUTE BOOK = 182
TRANSFORMATION = 183

THE POLICE = 93
POLICEMEN = 92

THE RACISM = 96
THE LEGACY = 86

THE LAW OF RETRIBUTION = 241
THEORY OF GONTIERISM = 241

THE S.A. P. = 69
THE S.O.B. = 69

THE BODY = 79
OF THE LAW = 69

TEMPLE = 71
MONEY = 72

THE S.O.B. = 69
THE TEARS = 96

TREE = 48
NEST = 58

TURF = 65
GRASS = 64

THE S.A.P = 69
THE BLITZ = 69

TREE = 48
EGGS = 38

TOXIC WASTE = 139
CHEMICAL REACTION = 139

THE S.A.P. CODE = 96

TIME = 47

THE MAFIOSA = 97

SOCIETY = 96

THE MAFIOSA = 97
FREEMASON = 96

THE MAFIOSA = 97
ITALIAN MAFIA = 96

THE MAFIOSA = 97
GOODFELLAS = 96

THE SAINT = 96
THE HALO = 69

LATIN DOGMA = 96
JUDICIAL CODE = 96

LATIN DOGMA = 96
MAFIA JUDGES = 96

LATIN DOGMA = 96
MIND SHIT = 96

THE COPS = 86
BLUE LIGHT = 96

THE COPS = 86
Big BROTHER = 86

TEARS = 63
WEPT = 64

TAMBO = 51
MANDELA = 50

TAMBO = 51
THE A.N.C. = 51

THE WIFE = 76
WOMAN = 66

THE HUMAN MIND = 130
PANDORA'S BOX = 129

TWO = 58
To TANGO = 57

TARIFFS = 79
TAXES = 69

TOBACCO IS = 87
ADDICTIVE = 77

TOBACCO IS ADDICTIVE = 164
IS TOBACCO ADDICTIVE? = 164

TOBACCO = 59
DANGER   = 49

THE KEY OF PETER = 159
WORD FOR WORD = 159

CROSS OF PETER = 159
CHRIST HIMSELF = 149

TEMPER = 77
JUSTICE = 87

THE CHAMP = 74

THE CLAY = 74

TYPICAL = 86
HUMOUR = 96

TYPICAL = 86
HO-HO-HO... HA-HA-HA = 96

TOY = 60
BOYS = 61

THE DOCTOR = 108
THE SKULL = 108

THE DOCTOR = 108
OPERATOR = 108

THE DOCTOR = 108
AIDS PATIENT = 118

TELEVISION IMAGE = 165
GHOST SOCIETY = 165

TELEVISION IMAGE = 165
MICRO SOFT-WARE = 165

TELEVISION IMAGE = 165
INTER-WEB & WEB-NET = 165

TELEVISION IMAGE = 165
COMPUTER-BRAIN = 155

TRAFFIC = 63
FUMES = 64

TRAFFIC = 63
OFFICER = 62

THAT = 49
BRAND = 39

THE SMOKE = 96
THE FUMES = 97

TREE = 48
RING = 48

TREE = 48
YEAR = 49

THE CONTROLLER = 165
THE THREE SIXES = 165

TWIST = 91
D.N.A. = 19

TWIST = 91
A HEAD = 19

THEORY = 91
IDEA = 19

THEORY = 91
MAGNETIC IDEA = 91

TOOL = 62
ROOM = 61

TIMBER = 67

CITY = 57

TIMBER = 67
TREES = 67

TREES = 67
WATER = 67

THE CHINESE = 96
TAI WANESE = 97

TUDOR = 78
HOUSE = 68

TUDOR HEAD = 96
BISHOP = 69

TUDOR HEAD = 96
THE QUEEN = 95

THE QUEEN = 95
TART = 59

TART = 59
WHORE = 69

TOMB OF GOD = 97
A PYRAMID = 87

THE SENATE = 97
PLAYBOY = 96

THE ARABIC = 67
LOGOS = 68

THE ARABIC = 67
LANGUAGE = 68

TEST = 64
CENTRE = 65

THE MONEY ORDER = 165
THE WORLD ORDER = 165

THE ALPHA AND THE OMEGA = 164
THE MAGNETIC ORDER = 165

TOLL = 59
TAXES = 69

THE HACKER = 79
RED TAPE = 69

THE HACKER = 79
STORY = 97

THE HACKER = 79
ALIEN MAN = 69

THE IMAM = 69
BISHOP = 69

THE IMAM = 69
THE BILAL = 69

THE IMAM = 69
KORAN = 59

THE LAVIS = 96

CHURCH IMAGE = 96

THE LAVIS = 96
MOSLEMS = 96

THE NEWS CODEX = 145
PSYCHOLOGY = 145

THE NEWS CODEX = 145
THE DEVIL'S KEY = 145

THE NEWS CODEX = 145
THE BOOK OF THE DEAD = 144

THE NEWS CODEX = 145
HEAVENLY BODIES = 146

THE NEWS CODEX = 145
NATURAL SCIENCE = 145

TABLETS = 79
TEXT = 69

TABLETS = 79
MAGNETS = 79

THE WHEEL = 86
TYRE = 68

TOY-GIRL = 106
PLAYBOY = 96

THE BOX = 74
TELLY = 74

THE TELE = 75
THE T.V. = 75

THE WHEEL = 86
of JUSTICE = 87

THE BALANCE OF EVIDENCE = 159
WORD FOR WORD = 159

THE BALANCE OF EVIDENCE = 159
LORD OF JUDGEMENT = 169

THE EVIDENCE OF BALANCE = 159
LOGO OF JUDGEMENT = 169

TO MIX = 81
POWDER = 81

TO MIX = 81
THE SAND = 71

THE CONGRESS = 133
GOVERNMENT = 133

THE DEATH AREA = 96
TOMBS = 69

TOWER = 81
Of BABYLON = 71

THE MIND KEY = 114
YIN AND YANG = 114

THE MIND KEY = 114

THE BUDDHA KEY = 114

THE MIND KEY = 114
SIX AND NINE = 113

THE MIND KEY = 114
HISTORICAL = 114

TRAILER = 83
AND HORSE = 84

TAKE-AWAY = 87
TEA-ROOM = 87

TAKE-AWAY = 87
STALE FOOD = 97

THE GAME = 59
Of PEOPLE = 69

THE EYE OF ISIS = 145
DAGNE AUD GULDVOG = 145

THE EYE OF ISIS = 145
NOSTRADAMUS = 145

TAR = 39
ROAD = 38

TO CURB = 79
THE LAW = 69

TO FREE = 69
SOCIETY = 96

TIME BOMB = 79
FAT BOY = 69

TIME BOMB = 79
FAT LADY = 69

U

UNITED = 73
NATION = 73

UNITED = 73
SACRIFICE = 73

UNITE = 69
UNTIE = 69

UNITE = 69
ECLIPSE = 69

UNITE = 69
ROMANCE = 69

UNIVERSAL FORCES = 187
ANGULAR MOMENTUM = 188

UNDER = 62
DOG = 26

URBAN = 56
HERO = 46

UNDER = 62
WORLD = 72

UNDER = 62
COVER = 63

UNDER = 62
POPE = 52

UNDER = 62
QUEEN = 62

UNDER = 62
YOU = 61

UNIFY = 75
MANIFOLD = 74

UN = 35
REAL = 36

UNREAL = 71
NEWS = 61

UN-CUT = 79
RED-TAPE = 69

UN-CUT = 79
STORY = 97

UNTRUE = 99
UPRIGHT = 99

UNTRUE = 99
JUDGEMENT = 99

UNTRUE = 99
JUDGES = 66

UNIQUE = 87
DIFFERENT = 87

UNIQUE = 87
PERSON = 87

UNIQUE = 87
JUSTICE = 87

UNIQUE = 87
VISION = 88

UNIQUE = 87
BEGOTTEN = 88

UNIQUE = 87
BLUE BLOOD = 88

UNPREDICTABLE = 130
PANDORA'S BOX = 129

UNPREDICTABLE = 130
PANDORA'S CAMERA = 129

UNDERTAKER = 117
THE GRAVE LAND = 117

UNDER = 62
DOOR = 52

UMUTHI = 92
MEDICINE = 62

UNDER = 62
ESTIMATE = 92

UPPER-CLASS = 130
THE INNER-BEING = 130

UPPER BEING = 113
DYING SUN = 113

UPPER BEING = 113
THE FACES OF GOD = 114

V

VEDAS = 51
INDIAN = 51

VEDAS = 51
EPICS = 52

VIRGIN = 79
GHOST = 69

VIRGIN = 79
WHORE = 69

VIRGIN = 79
MOTHER = 79

VITAL = 64
ENERGY = 74

VINE = 50
WINE = 51

VOCAL = 53
VOICE = 54

VOICES = 73
SOUND = 73

VOICES = 73
DIALOGUE = 74

VOICES = 73
TALKING = 74

VINEGAR = 76
HONEY = 67

VIGINAS = 73
PENIS = 63

VIRGIN MARY = 158
MOTHER MARY = 158

VIRGIN MARY = 158
THE MOTHER OF GOD = 159

VIEW = 59
BEHOLDER = 69

VIEW = 59
DIRECT = 59

VIEW = 59
BLIND MAN = 69

VIRUS = 89
PARASITE = 89

VOTE = 62
BALLOT = 62

VAMPIRES = 103
HUMAN BODY = 103

VAMPIRES = 103
BIG BROTHER = 104

VAMPIRES = 103
THE DEMONS = 103

VAMPIRES = 103
THE AIDS DEATH = 104

VAMPIRES = 103
EXORCISED = 102

VITAL = 64
PARTS = 74

VITAL-LIFE = 96
SELF LOVE = 96

VLAK = 46
PLAAS = 49

VOTE = 62
VETO = 62

VIRGIN = 79
JUNGLE = 69

VERY GOOD = 111
WITCHCRAFT = 111

VERY GOOD WITCHCRAFT = 222
THE FIRST BORN OF THE DEAD =
222

VISIT = 79
MOTHER = 79

VILLAIN = 79
BANDITS = 69

VISION OF LIFE = 141
JESUS CHRIST = 151

VADER EN = 69
SEUN = 59

VACCINATION = 130
HIPPOCRATES = 130

W

WORD OF GOD = 107
MATHEMATICAL = 106

WORD OF GOD = 107
ARITHMETIC = 106

WHITE = 65
LIGHT = 56

WORDS = 79
LETTER = 80

WORDS = 79
SECULAR = 79

WORDS = 79
STORY = 97

WORDS = 79
MESSAGE = 69

WHOLE = 63
NUMBER = 73

WAR = 42
MARCH = 43

WHITE = 65
WOMAN = 66

WAR = 42
LOCK = 41

WET = 48
DRY = 47

WO- = 38
MAN = 28

WO- = 38
MO = 28

WANING = 68
WAXING = 78

WOLF = 56
WOOL = 65

WOLVES = 96
FOXES = 69

WOLVES = 96
PEDIGREE = 69

WOLVES = 96
ALSATIANS = 96

WEE-WEE = 66
URINE = 67

WEE-WEE = 66
SUGAR = 66

WISDOM = 83
THE MIND = 73

WISDOM = 83
THE BUDDHA = 73

WISDOM = 83
DOWISM = 83

WISDOM = 83
MONKEY = 83

WISDOM = 83
ARSE-HOLE = 83

WATCH = 55
CLOCK = 44

WAR = 42
GUN = 42

WHOLE = 63
SUM = 53

WHORE = 69
HOUSE = 68
WHORE = 69
PLAYBOY = 96

WHORE = 69
TART = 59

WHORE = 69
VIRGIN = 79

WHORE = 69
NUNS = 68

WORLD = 72
RACE = 27

WITHIN = 83
OUTSIDE = 93

WATER = 67
VINEGAR = 76

WEAPON = 74
TACTICS = 75

WORLD = 72
ROUND = 72

WORLD = 72
ORIGIN = 72

WORLD = 72
MAGNETIC = 72

WORLD = 72
UTOPIA = 82

WORLD = 72
HITLER = 72

WORLD – 72
MONEY = 72

WELL = 52
TOLD = 51

WORLD WISDOM = 155
THE BEGINNING AND END = 156

WAR-LIKE = 79
ANIMALS = 69

WALLET = 73
MONEY = 72

WHITE = 65
RHINO = 64

WAKE = 40

DREAM = 41

WALL = 48
OF FIRE = 38

WORLD = 72
WIDE WEB = 71

WITCH = 63
HUNT = 63

WITCH-CRAFT = 111
SORCERIES = 111

WITCH-CRAFT = 111
INSANITY = 111

WITCH-CRAFT = 111
COMPUTER = 111

WITCH DOCTOR = 138
MEDICINE WOMAN = 128

WOODS = 76
COMPASS = 86

WOODS = 76
TREES = 67

WOODS = 76
TIMBER = 67

WILD = 48
GARDEN = 49

WILD = 48
SEX = 48
WILD = 48
SON = 48

WILD = 48
FIRE = 38

WILD = 48
AFRICA = 38

WOMAN = 66
& SONG = 55

WHOLE = 63
TRACK = 53

WHITE = 65
LAWS = 55

WHITE = 65
RULE = 56

WASTE = 68
TRON = 67

WASTE = 68
BASKET = 58

WILD = 48
COAST = 58

WAVE-THEORY = 142
CROSS OF TIME = 142

WAVE-THEORY = 142
RELATIVITY = 141

WAVE PHOTON = 139
ELECTRICAL WAVE = 139

WAVE PHOTON = 139
SOLAR ENERGY = 139

WAVE PHOTON = 139
LIGHT ENTITY = 149

WAVE PHOTON = 139
CHRIST HIMSELF = 149

WAVE PHOTON = 139
HOLLYWOOD = 129

WIG = 39
ROBE = 40

WHITE = 65
PAPER = 56

WOOD = 57
IRON = 56

WOOD = 57
HUMAN = 57

WHITE = 65
GREY = 55

WINNING = 90
LETTER = 80

WAX = 48
FIRE = 38

WORLD = 72
REST = 62

WOOD = 57
BORER = 58

WE WANT = 86
JUSTICE = 87

WATCHES = 79
THE TIME = 80

'WHEN WE' = 78
from RHODESIA = 79

'WE HAVE...' = 64
a LIFT-OFF = 74

WONDER = 79
STEVIE = 80

WONDER = 79
BLIND-MAN = 69

WHITE = 65
HORSE = 65

WISH = 59
DESIRE = 60

WINE = 51
CELLAR = 51

WINDOW = 88
VISION = 88

WHITE = 65
WEDDING = 66

WINDS = 69
OF CHANGE = 59

WINDS OF CHANGE = 128
NELSON MANDELA = 129

WINDS OF AFRICA = 128
PANDORA'S BOX = 129

WINDS OF AFRICA = 128
PEOPLE DYING = 128

WHO'S = 65
The BOSS = 55
WHO'S = 65
THE BAAS = 56

WICK = 46
FLAMES = 56

WICKS = 65
FLAMES = 56

WASP = 59
STING = 69

WOOD = 57
WORK = 67

WOOD = 57
CITY = 57

WEB-NET = 69
WWW = 69

WEB-NET = 69
INTER-WEB = 96

WEB-NET = 69
HUMAN NET = 96

WEB-NET = 69
COBWEBS = 69

WEB-NET = 69
BINARY = 69

WWW CODE = 96
BINARY-CODE = 96

WEB-NET NEWS = 130

NEW VISION = 130

WEB-NET NEWS = 130
TELEVISION = 130

WILLIAM = 79
SMITH = 69

WILLIAM TELL = 128
THE THIRD EYE = 127

WORKING = 97
For PEANUTS = 96

WORKING = 97
For POPCORN = 97

WEIRD = 59
HABITS = 59

X

XMAS = 57
BIRTH = 57

XMAS = 57
TIME = 47

X-RAY = 68
THE BONE = 69

Y

YIN = 48
YANG = 47

YOD HE = 57
VAU HE = 57

YOUNG = 82
MAN = 28

YESTERDAY = 122
TODAY AND TOMORROW = 221

YIN & YANG = 95
BIOLOGY = 85

YIN AND YANG = 114
SIX AND NINE = 113

YIN AND YANG = 114
GENETIC CODING = 115

YEN = 44
MARK = 43

YEAST = 70

STARCH = 69

YEAR = 49
MODEL = 49

YEAR = 49
CYCLE = 48

YEARS = 68
CALENDAR = 58

YEARS = 68
Of SCIENCE = 58

YEAR TIME = 96
Y2K CALENDAR = 96

YAMAHA = 49
BICYCLE = 59

Z

ZERO = 64
CENTRE = 65

ZERO = 64
ENERGY = 74

ZERO = 64
TAKE-OFF = 64

ZOO = 56
CITY = 57

ZOO = 56
HUMAN = 57

ZULU = 80
THE BEAST = 80

ZULU = 80
AFRIKAANS = 80

ZULU = 80
KING SHAKA = 81

ZULU = 80
STOP = 70

ZERO = 64
ORIFICE = 65

ZERO = 64
FINITE = 63

ZERO = 64
GODLY = 63

ZEUS = 71
DEITIES = 71

RELATIVE TOA

69	96	96	96
A ALIEN CODE	A BABY CENTER	FIXED BLOOD	OPEN HANDS
A ALIEN RACE	A BABY TOKEN	FIXED CYCLE	OPENED UP
A BELL DOME	A BABYALPHABET	FLAME OF FIRE	OPENS HAND
A BONE CELL	A BANK EXCHANGE	FLAT RENT	ORGAN HOME
A BONE LIFE	A BIBLE ALPHABET	FLAT SANDS	ORGAN KEY
A BUSH HEAD	A CAKE DOCTOR	FLOOR BUG	ORGANISM
A CLEAN NAME	A CHEMICAL KEY	FLOOR MAP	OSCILLATE
A COW HAND	A CHOIR BOY	FOETUS BAG	OT NT CODE
A DAGGA TREE	A CONGOLESE	FOOD DEFICIT	OUMAS HAND
A DOG TAIL	A CROSS BAR	FOOD MESS	OUMAS RACE
A DOLLY	A CYCLE OF GOD	FOR RENT	OUR NEW
A DOM PAS	A DAGGA TREE BASE	FORCED LIES	OUR SIN
A DUAL BABY	A DEAD RITUAL	FORM RAY	OUT HOLE
A FREE COKE	A DEATH RISK	FOUND CHILD	OUT LINE
A GENITAL	A DIVINE LIFE	FREE BOOKS	OUT MIND
A HERETIC	A DOCUMENT	FREE FACT FILE	OUT OF ADAM
A LAB GRAVE	A DOG TAIL HALF	FREE HOUR	OUT OF EGG
A MAN LANDED	A DOOR FRAME	FREE LOOT	OUT OF IDEA
A MARKET	A DRESSING	FREE MA SON	OUTER BACK
A NAIL BOMB	A DUPLICATED	FREE MARKS	OVER COME
A NANNY	A FLASH BACK LIFE	FREE MEDICINE	OVER FIELD
A NEW GAME	A FLAVOUR	FREE PLASMA	OVER OHM
A NOVICE	A FREE ROMAN	FREE RIGHT	OVER RIDE
A PILLAR	A GENTLEMEN	FREE SENSE	OVULATE
A PLANET	A GESTURE	FREE SHOT	PAGAD QIBLA DATA
A RADIO BAND	A GIANT BRAIN	FREE TAKING	PAID FOR RACE
A REGION	A HAND STOCK	FREE VOTE	PAINTED RED
A ROCK BAND	A HIERARCHY	FREEDOM BIBLE	PAPPAS RACE
A SAFE PLACE	A HIGHER MIND	FREEDOM DAY	PARALLELS
A SCOOP	A HOLY EYE	FRESH FOOD	PARKLANDS
A SCREW	A HOLY IMAGE	FROM A BOOK	PARTIAL ADAM
A SELF GAME	A IMPULSE	FROM BRAIN	PARTIAL IDEA
A SERIEL	A INNER EYE	FROM OFFICE	PASS KEY
A STOCK	A INNER IMAGE	FROM SET	PAST MIND
A SUMO	A JOB MARKET	FROM SPACE	PAUPERS
A TAG LINE	A LABIA MINORA	FRONT END	PEACE FAMILY
A TOTAL	A LACK OF TIME	FUCKLESS	PEACE ONLY
A WAR GOD	A LIFE RECORD	FULL RANGE	PERFECT END
ACHILLES	A LIGHT ANGLE	FUNERALS	PEROXIDE
ADAM APPLE	A LOVE HOME	FUNKYS	PERPLEX
AFRICA LAND	A LOVE KEY	FURTHER	PHOBIC BOOK
AFRIGHT	A MAD REPLAY	FUTILE END	PHOBIC WIFE
AGRARIAN	A MAFIA BONDING	GAS CHAMBERS	PIANO KEY
AIR LOCK	A MAGNET EYE	GATES BRAIN	PICKING HAND
ALICE HEAD BAND	A MAGNET IMAGE	GAY CAMPING	PICTURED
AMINO ACID	A MARKET CODE	GAYS BRAIN	PIETS RACE
ANIMALS	A MARKET RACE	GEAR CENTRE	PIGEON PIE
ANNUS	A MARTYR	GENETIC AIDS	PINK BALLS
APPENDAGE	A MASKED BITCH	GENETIC NAME	PLACE OF DEATH
ARCH ANGEL	A MASKED BOY	GENETIC SEED	PLANET AIR
AREAL LIFE	A MASKED FEMALE	GENTLE NAME	PLANET CALL
AS LORD	A MASKED LADY	GERMAN ADOLF	PLANET MAN

ASH BOX	A MOB BONDING	GERMAN BALANCE	PLAY BITCH
AUDIOS	A NAKED WORD	GERMAN DEATH	PLAY BOY
BABY ANGEL	A NEW BALL GAME	GERMAN JEW	PLAY LADY
BABY BELIEF	A NEW HAND GAME	GERMAN SS	PLAYED MAGIC
BABY FABRIC	A NEW LOOK	GERONIMO	PLAYED NAME
BABY MATE	A NIGHTMARE	GHOST CODE	PLAYERS
BABY MEAT	A NUCLEUS	GHOST HAND	PLUNGEDBACK
BACK BOOT	A PEACE CENTER	GHOST RACE	POLICE CHILD
BACK DEALING	A PEACE TOKEN	GIZA COFFIN	POLICE FIELD
BACK DOOR	A PECULIAR BAG	GIZA GRAVE	POLICE LAW
BACK STAGE	A PENIS LIFE	GIZA LEGACY	POLICE WAGE
BACK TO BACK	A PETERPAN	GO BETWEEN	POOR COCK
BACK TO ICE	A PINEALGLAND	GOD LEARNT	POOR LIFE
BACKS NAME	A PLANET CODE	GOD LIKE NAME	PORT HAND
BALANCED CODE	A PLANET RACE	GOD OF ATOM	POST CARD
BALANCED HAND	A PLANT LIFE	GOD OF DANGER	POST DATA
BALLS END	A PLUS COED	GOD OF GREEN	POST DOG
BANANA BONE	A PRESCRIBE	GOD SHADOW	POST LIE
BANANA CHILD	A REAR LOOK	GOD STOP	POWERS
BANANA FIELD	A RED HOUSE	GODS AND MEN	PRAYED HAND
BANANA LAW	A ROMAN ONE	GODS DIENS	PRAYER AGE
BANDITS	A ROSTER	GODS DNA LIFE	PRAYER ID
BARONS	A SECOND EYE	GODS OF ASIA	PRE DATED END
BECAME FOOD	A SECOND IMAGE	GODS OF ASIA	PRE PAID BY
BECAME MIND	A SKY LINE	GODS WINE	PRIMEVAL
BEEN CAST	A SON OF GOD	GOLD BELTS	PRIMUS
BEER CIDER	A STOCK CODE	GOLD BERG DATA	PROCEEDING
BEER MATE	A SUB MACHINE	GOLD SCANDLE	PROCLAIMED
BEER TEAM	A SUMO RACE	GOLD STAR	PROJECTED
BEGIN A ECHO	A TEACHING MAN	GOLDEN ANGEL	PUBLISHED
BEGIN A HER	A TOTAL CODE	GOLDEN BELT	PUMPING
BEGIN A LAND	A TRAINED MK	GOLFER NAME	PYMANDER
BEGIN LIFE	A TREE OF GOD	GOOD FELLAS	QUARTS
BEHOLDER	A WEATHER FACE	GRAMMA MARK	QUASARS
BELLS IDEA	A WHITE BABY	GRAPHS CODE	QUEEN BIDS
BENDED IMAGE	A WHITE BIBLE	GRAVE MARK	QUEENS BID
BENDED NAKED	A WHITE BREAD	GRAVEL LAND	QUEER BABY
BENSON	A WHITE MOB	GREAT RANGE	QUEER BIBLE
BIBLE ANGEL	A WHOLE LIFE	GREY KEY	QUEER DAY
BIBLE ANGLE	ABBA GOVERNED	GROOMED ADAM	QUEER MAFIA
BIBLE BELIEF	ACT DEFINITE	GROOMED IDEA	QUEER MOB
BIBLICAL ADAM	ACTIVE CHILD	GROUPS	QUEUE CODE
BIBLICALS	ACTIVE FIELD	GROWN ADAM	QUICK ANT
BIG TOP	ACTIVE LAW	GROWN DNA	QUICK EYE
BINARY	ACTIVE OHM	GROWN IDEA	QUICK IMAGE
BISHOP	ACTUAL DEATH	GUARANTEED	QUIET ACT
BLACK BARS	ADAM CHRIST	GUIDED HANDS	QUIET CAT
BLACK BLUE	ADAM EVE AND GOD	GUN BLAST	QURAN MECCA
BLACK BOARD	ADAM IS ALIVE	HALF HAND GIFT	QURANIC AGE
BLACK BOW	ADAMS FATHER	HAND CART RACE	QURANIC ID
BLACK BUDDHA BACK	ADD NOTHING	HAND DATED IMAGE	RACE BACK TO
BLACK CORD	ADDED START	HAND FIXING	RACE CART RACE
BLACK HABIT	ADOLFS MATE	HAND GRAPHS	RACE REMAINED
BLACK HOBO	ADOLFS TEAM	HAND GUN CODE	RACE WAR CODE
BLACK HOLE	ADOLFS VICE	HAND MAPPER	RACE WAR RACE

BLACK LINE	ADVANCES CODE	HAND MIXER	RACIAL NAMES
BLACK MIND	ADVERT DATA	HAND SEALED END	RAM SAI AUM
BLACK ROBE	ADVERT LIE	HANDLING CODE	RARE RED CODE
BLANK BLACK	AFRICAN BRAIN	HANGING FEET	RARE RED RED
BLENDED END	AFRIGHT CODE	HANGING FIELD	RATIONS
BLENDED IN	AGELESS MAN	HANGING LAW	RAW CHEMICAL
BLIND MAN	AGENCIES NAME	HE IS LESS	RAY FORM
BLITZ	AGRARIANCODE	HEAD OF A LIGHT	RAY SIX
BLOT ABLE	AIR PASSAGE	HEAD OF HUMAN	RC DIAMETER
BLUNT	AIR ROOT	HEAD OF MOON	RC DISTANCE
BOLTABLE	AIR STOCK	HEADING CRIME	RC DOCTOR
BORNABLE	AIR WAYS	HEADS OFFERED	RE ARRIVE
BRACKETED	ALLAH IS ALLAH	HEART RATE	RE SOLVE
BREAD MEAT	ALLAH IS ONE	HEIGHT ANGLE	RE SURFACE
BRINGS	AMERICAS BASE	HELP LESS	RE TESTED
BROKER	AMERICAS CODE	HELPLESS	RE UNION
BUSH ADAM	AMERICAS HAND	HER MOULD	RE UNITED
BUSH DNA	AMERICAS RACE	HER ORIFICE	READ ARTICLE
BUSH IDEA	AN ACTOR ACT	HERBIE BEETLE	REALISTIC
CALL BOX	AN ELEPHANT	HERODS CODE	RECASTING
CALL HOME	ANIMATION	HERODS RACE	RECORD NAME
CALL KEY	ANNOINTED	HIDDEN DEVIL	RECOUNT
CALM MIND	APHRODITE	HIDDEN DOOR	RECYCLE ALL
CAMEL EYE	APPEND MIND	HIDDEN EARTH	RECYCLE AREA
CAMEL IMAGE	APPLIANCES	HIDDEN FORM	RECYCLE BIN
CAMELOT	APPREHENDED	HIDDEN LAST	RECYCLE PI
CAMERA MAN	ARAB CROSS	HIDDEN PRIDE	RECYCLE SEA
CAR RADIO	ARE MAGNETIC	HIDDEN SHIP	RECYCLING
CAR TIME	ARM PITS	HIM TO HER	RED BISHOP
CAREERS	ARRIVE IN	HIRE BLACK RACE	RED BISHOP
CASH CHANGE	ARYAN MODE	HIS DESIRE	RED CENT HALF
CASH GOLD	AS PART OF	HIS EGO NAME	RED COAL FIRE
CASH PIECE	ASSOCIATED	HIS GOAL AREA	RED FOR A GANG
CATCH ONE	ATLANTIS	HIS LIFE CALL	RED FOR MAFIA
CATPATH	AUM SAI RAM	HIS VOW	RED FOR MOB
CENTRED	AUTO GARAGE	HITLER ACT	RED FOR PEACE
CHAMBERS	AUTO MATE	HIV PRICK	RED GAS WAR
CHANGE CASH	AUTO NET	HIV VACCINE	RED GRAPHS
CHARTS	AUTO TEAM	HOLD ON CALL	RED IS BLIND
CHATTEL	AVOIDING FACE	HOLDING HAND	RED IS GOOD
CHECK MATF	AVOIDS DATA	HOLY CHILD	RED IS HOME
CHECKMATE	AVOIDS GOD	HOLY CHIP	RED IS KING
CHEWING	AVOIDS LIE	HOLY FIELD	RED IS MOM
CIRCLES	AWOKEN RACE	HOLY LAW	RED ISNT BAD
CLEARED OF	BABIES FATHER	HOME IS BASE	RED KNIGHT
CLIMBING	BABY GIGGLES	HOME SOIL	RED KNIGHT
CLUCKS	BABY MATE HAND	HOMELESS	RED LAND FIRE
COACH MATE	BABY MYTH	HORSE CASH	RED MIXER
COACH TEAM	BABY RAT RACE	HORSE LAND	RED SUIT
COAL FIRE	BACK BRACKETS	HOUSE CALL	RED TAPE BASE
COBWEBS	BACK DEALING RACE	HOWEVER	RED TAPE CODE
COCK DOME	BACK DOORCODE	HUMAN ANGEL	RED WHORE
CODED DEATH	BACK GROUND	HUMAN ANGLE	REDEEMS RACE
CODEDCHANGE	BACK MOMMY	HUMAN HIV	REFLECT RED
COILING	BACK MOTHER	HUMAN MATE	REFOCUSED
COLD EYE	BACK TRACK DATA	HUMAN MEAT	RELATE TO

COLD IMAGE	BACK TRACK LIE	HUMAN NET	RELIVING
COME CHEAP	BACKROUTE	HUMAN PIN	REMAIN BONE
CONGELLA	BAD GATHERING	HUMAN RAT	REMAIN CHILD
CONRADIE	BAD MEMORY	HUMAN TEAM	REMAIN LAW
COOL CAT	BAIL MONEY	HUMAN VICE	REMAINS BACK
COOL KID	BALANCE ALL AIDS	HUMANTEAM	REMIX CODE
CORNS	BALANCE ALL MAGIC	HUMBLE IMAGE	REMIX RACE
CREMATED	BALANCE ALL NAME	HUMOUR	REMIX RED
CRIME EDGE	BALANCE OF NICK	HYDROGEN	RENUMBER
CURRI	BALANCING NAME	I AM PARADISE	REOFFERER
CURVE	BALLS IN HAND	I AM PERFECT	REPLAY ADAM
DADS CLUE	BANANA BREAD NAME	I AM SELECTED	REPLAYS
DADS DEFEAT	BANANA FIELD HAND	I REMAIN CAIN	REPLAYS
DADS KEY	BANANA PLANT	I REST ALL	REPULSE
DADSJOKE	BANK MARKET	I SEEK ALSO	RESACRIFICE
DAGGA ATOM	BANK STOCK	I SEEK MONAD	RESELECTED
DAGGA GREEN	BANKING A RAND	I SEEK TIME	RESERVED
DAGWOOD	BANKING AFRICA	I STARTED	RETURN
DAM FULL	BANKING CHANGE	I TALIAN BREAD	REVERED IDEA
DARWIN	BANKING DEATH	I TALIAN DRAG	REVERSED
DATED IMAGE	BANKING GOLD	I TALIAN MAFIA	RHETORIC
DEAD IN LIFE	BANTU AFRICA	I TALIAN PIE	RICHARD GERE
DEADSEA BIBLE	BANTU CHANGE	ICE DWELLER	RICKSHA RACE
DEATH CASH	BANTU GOLD	IDEA OF LIGHT	RIGHT HATE
DEATH LAND	BANTUS DNA	IDEA OF PAST	RIGHT ONE
DEEP FILL	BANTUS IDEA	IDIOTIC CODE	RISK ANGLE
DEFENCE CODE	BAR CHANGERS	IM A NUMBER	RISK MATE
DESCRIBED	BARONS CODE	IM A SACRIFICE	RISK TEAM
DIE BROKE	BARREL HOLE	IM CROSS	RISK TEN
DIET MEAL	BASIS LOGIC	IM DUIWEL	ROAD SIDE EDGE
DIGITABLE	BEATLES LIFE	IM ELEVATED	ROBOT CARD
DIGITAL CD	BEERS LEGEND	IM FOREIGN	ROBOT DOG
DISECTED	BEERS MONAD	IM IN A CIRCLE	ROBOT GOD
DOMKRAG	BEETHOVEN	IM JESUS	ROBOT LIE
DOODLAND	BEETLE MONAD	IM LUCIFER	ROBOT MEGA
DRAG NET	BEGIN LAUNCH	IM MESSIAH	ROCK DANGER
DRAG TEAM	BEGIN SOLID	IM MUHAMMAD	ROMES GOD
DRAMA LIFE	BEING SOLID	IM SIMPLE	ROOT MAN
DRAMATIC	BELIEVED LIFE	IM SON GOD	ROSARY
DRUGS	BELOW TEN	IM TALKING	ROTARIAN
DUAL LAND	BERLIN CHILD	IM THE GOOD	RUBBER ARK
DUG UP	BERLIN LAW	IM THE KING	RUBBER BABY
DYNAMIC	BERLIN OHM	IM THE MOM	RUBBER MOB
DYNAMIC	BERTRAMS	IM THE OMEGA	RUGBY END
ECLIPSE	BEST ANIMAL	IM WISER	RULES AT
EGO DEFENCE	BEST CIRCLE	IMAGE REJECT	RULES OF
EL NINO	BIBLE MYTH	IMAGE TO GOD	RUMBLING
ENCIRCLE	BIBLE TITLE	IMENERGY	RYTHMIC
ENCODED A HEAD	BIBLE TYPE	IMITATES	SACRED BODY
ENCODED ADAM	BILLETED CODE	IMMUTABLE	SACRED CHANT
ENCODED DNA	BINARY CODE	IMPOSES	SAFE CENTER
ENCODED EGG	BINARY CODE	IN COMMON	SAFE STATE
ENCODED IDEA	BIONICAL ECHO	IN DIAN GODS	SALVAGE A MAN
ENHANCES	BISHOP CODE	IN DIAN PATH	SAME FATHER
ENJOY	BISHOP HAND	IN FLATED SEA	SAME FEELING
EYE TIE	BISHOP RACE	IN FORMAT	SAME SCIENCE

FAILED AGAIN
FAILED LIFE
FAMILIAR
FARM LAND
FASTER
FAT BITCH
FAT BOY
FAT LADY
FATIGUE
FAULTED
FEALTY
FEEDING IDEA
FIGHTS
FILED NAME
FILLING
FINAL CODE
FINAL HAND
FINAL RACE
FINANCIAL
FIRED CODE
FIRED GAS
FIRED HAND
FIXED EDGE
FIXED ICI
FIXING
FLASHER
FOOD CABIN
FOOT AGE
FOR BABY
FOR HIM
FOR MAFIA
FOR PEACE
FORKS
FOUNDED
FOYER
FREE EYE
FREE GOAL
FREE IMAGE
FREE LANCE
FREE TO
FULL DAM
GAIN BALANCE
GAS FIRED
GAS GUN
GAY CHILD
GAY LAW
GEAR BALANCE
GEAR CHANGE
GEAR MAX
GET UP
GHOST
GLO MAIL
GOAT GOD
GOD SAW
GOD SEEN
GOD WAS

BLACK BASE LINE
BLACK BLUE RED
BLACK CODE LINE
BLACK HOLE RACE
BLACK IN SPACE
BLACK MAN HOLD
BLACK NOBLES
BLACK RED LINE
BLACK RINGS
BLACK WATER
BLAME OF GUN
BLAME OF SELF
BLAME OF SIN
BLAME OF WAR
BLANK OUT
BLATANT LIE
BLINDLESS
BLITZ CODE
BLOOD BUY
BLOOD CRAFT
BLOOD CYCLE
BLOOD FILLED
BLOOD OF RACE
BLOOD OF RED
BLOOD SEX
BLOOD SON
BLOOD TRADE
BLOOD TREE
BLUE LIGHT
BLUNT HAND
BODY GRIP
BOERE HEAD NAME
BOLTABLE CODE
BOLTABLE RACE
BOMB DUST
BONDING A BABY
BONDING CASH
BONDING LAND
BONE CLUES
BONES HOME
BONES KEY
BOOK GRAVE
BOOK LEGACY
BORN MONAD
BORNABLE CAIN
BORNABLE RACE
BOW DOWN
BOXED BODY
BOYZ CALL
BOYZ MAN
BRACKETED CODE
BRAIN DEALING
BRAIN FLUID
BRAIN FROM
BRANCH GRIP
BREATHS IN

IN FRONT
IN MERIDIAN
IN NOTES
IN OFFERER
IN PROSE
IN SIDE FIELD
IN SIDE LAW
IN SINCERE
IN SOUND
IN STONE
IN TEL CHIP
IN THE BUDDHA
IN THE HOLE
IN THE MIND
IN TURN
IN UNION
IN VOICES
IN WARD BASE
IN WARD CODE
IN WARD RACE
INDEX FOOD
INDEX LINE
INDEX MIND
INDIAN BRIDGE
INDIAN HEAD BASE
INDIAN RED HEAD
INDIAS BUDDHA
INDIAS FOOD
INDICATED HAND
INFANT LIFE
INFLATED AREA
INNER CHILD
INNER CHIP
INNER FIELD
INNER LAW
INNER OHM
INSIDE BITE
INSIDE BONE
INSIDE CHIP
INTEL FIELD
INTEL LAW
INTER BUG
INTER DATE
INTER DAY
INTER MAP
INTERWEB
IS LAMIC BIBLE
IS LAMIC MOB
ISCOR ARM
ISCOR CELL
ISCOR LIFE
ISLAMIC MAFIA
ISUZU
ITALIAN BABY
ITALIAN BIBLE
ITALIAN MOB

SAME STAR
SANTAM BANK
SARCOMA DATA
SATANISM
SATANISM
SAVOUR
SCANDALLING
SCARY MOB
SCHNAPPS
SCHOOL ACT
SCIENCE BALANCE
SCIENCE CHANGE
SCIENCE DEATH
SCREEN LIFE
SEA COTTAGE
SEA GULLS
SEA RESCUE
SEA TEMPLE
SEARCH IN A HEAD
SEE EVIDENCE
SEE POLIO
SEED GROW
SEED IN HOLE
SEED IN MIND
SEEING MODE
SEEING UP
SELECTED END
SELECTED IN
SELF BORNE
SELF EYES
SELF IMAGES
SELF LOVE
SELF REGAIN
SELFISH HEAD
SEMI CANALS
SEMI CIRCLE
SET FORM
SEX ABUSE
SEX JOIN
SEXIST
SHAKE EARTH
SHAKES NAME
SHAMAN FOOD
SHAMAN LIAR
SHAMAN MIND
SHARK ANGLE
SHARK MATE
SHARK MEAT
SHARK NET
SHARK TEAM
SHELL HOLE
SIDE LINES
SIMPLE DEAL
SIMPLE LEAD
SKI BOATS
SKIP A HOLE

GODS ACT	BRIDGED DOOM	JAIL BREAK CODE	SKIP A LINE
GODS CAT	BRIDGED MONAD	JAPANESE AREA	SKIP HOME
GOES IN	BRIDGED TIME	JAPANESE PI	SKY HOME
GOLD CASH	BRIDGES A LAND	JAPANS EYE	SKY KEY
GOLD LAND	BRIDGES LIFE	JESTERS	SKYISM
GOOD CALL	BRIDGING GOD	JEW CABALA BALANCE	SLAG HUIS
GOOD CASE	BRIGHT CELL	JEW FATHER	SLOW CODE
GOOD MAN	BRIGHT LIFE	JEW SCIENCE	SLOW RACE
GRANTED	BRINGS CODE	JEW STAR	SMALL ANGEL
GRAPHS	BROKEN A MOB	JEWS ANGEL	SMALL ANGLE
GREEN ABLE	BROKEN CASH	JEWS ANGLE	SMALL DOT
GREEN DAGGA	BROKEN ECHO	JEWS NET	SMALL TEAM
GRIPS	BROKEN LAND	JEWS TEAM	SMASHED CODE
GUIDED IDEA	BROKER CODE	JOIN BLOOD	SMASHED HAND
HADES LIFE	BROKER HAND	JOIN CYCLE	SMASHED RACE
HALF BOY	BUFFALO SEED	JOIN CYCLE	SMURFS
HALF CENT	BUILDING HEAD	JOIN EVIL	SMURFS
HALF FEMALE	BURGLED RACE	JOIN SEX	SNAKE PARK
HALF FISH	BUSH BODY	JOINERY	SNORING
HALF SELF	BUSH DOVE	JUDASISM	SOCCER NAME
HAND DEFENCE	BUSH HERO	JUDGE BRUCE	SOCIETY
HAND GIFT	BUSH LOGIC	JUDGE DANGER	SOIL HOME
HAND GUN	BUSH PIPE	JUDGE NOT	SOIL KEY
HAND WAR	C OUNTEND	JUDGES ARK	SOIL LOCK
HANDED NAME	C SHARP ECHO	JUDGES BIBLE	SOIL MOM
HANG TEN	CALL OF MONAD	JUDGES DAY	SOLID BEING
HAVENS	CALL OF THE DEAD	JUDGES DRAG	SOLID UP
HELP CALL	CALL OF TIME	JUDGES MAP	SOOTHS
HELP MAN	CALL ON HOLD	JUDICIAL CODE	SPACE EARTH
HEMP BASE	CALLING CHANGE	JUDICIAL HAND	SPACE MASS
HEMP RED	CALLING DEATH	JUDICIAL RACE	SPACE SHIP
HERO END	CANCERS NAME	JUDICIAL RACE	SPECIAL CASH
HERODS	CANT STAND	JUMBO JET	SPECIAL LAND
HEROIN	CAPACITY HEAD	JUMPED BASE	SPECIAL SAFE
HIGH PLACE	CAPSULES	JUMPED CODE	SPEECH CAPABLE
HIGH PU	CAPTAIN LIFE	JUMPED RACE	SPEED MONAD
HIGHLY	CAR ENERGY	JUNGLE DANCE	SPEED TIME
HIRE A MAN	CAR PARTS	JUNK FOOD	SPEEDABLE RACE
HIRE BLACK	CAR RADIO CODE	JUST LAID	SPINDLE BACK
HIRE IT	CARBON BLOCK	KAFFIR BOOM	SPINK BASE
HIS BANANA	CARCINOMAS	KAFFIR BRIDGE	SPINK CODE
HIS BIRD	CARRIED AFRICA	KAFFIR DOGS	SPINS DNA
HIS SEED	CARRIED CHANGE	KAFFIR GODS	SPIRAL EDGE
HIV BABY	CARRIED DEATH	KAFFIR KNIFE	SPLITABLE
HIV BUG	CARRIED GOLD	KAFFIR PATH	SPONGY
HIV DAY	CARTEL MODE	KAFFIRS LIE	SS STAR
HOLD A PAGE	CASH CARRY	KEY BONES	STABILISE
HOLD BABY	CASH CENTRE	KEY LESS	STAGGERS
HOLD MAFIA	CASH CHANGE HAND	KEY PART	STAGNANT
HOLD MOB	CASH LINKS	KEYMAN CODE	STALE ANGLE
HOLY I	CASH TODAY	KING LESS	STALE MATE
HOME CALL	CASH TOKEN	KINGS CHILD	STALE MEAT
HOT TEA	CAT WALK AREA	KINGS LAW	STALEMATE
HOWARD	CATHOLICAREA	KNIGHT CODE	STAMINAS
HUBBELS	CATS GRAVE	KNOW LEDGE	STAR BALANCE
HUSBAND	CELEBRATING	KOOL KIDS	STAR DEATH

I BELIEVE
I PRAY
I REMAIN
I VOW
I WORD
ICE RINK
ID INDEX
IDIOMS
IDIOTIC
IM DOOM
IM ELATED
IM JOHN
IM MONAD
IM OMEN
IM THE DEAD
IM THE MA
IM TIME
IN VAIN
IN WARD
INDIAN HEAD
INDICATED
INK PEN
INWARD
IRON AGE
IS ALIEN
IS GONE
IS GOOD
IS MOM
JACKETS
JAIL A LAW
JAIL BREAK
JAIL TAKE
JAILED MAN
JAMBOREE
JAPAN RACE
JASPER
JEHOVAH
JIGSAW
JIGSAW
JOYS
JUDICIAL
JUNGLE
KELE BONE
KEY CALL
KEYMAN
KNIGHT
LAND BALANCE
LAND CHANGE
LAND PIECE
LAUGHABLE
LEARNS
LEATHER
LEE MONAD
LEGAL FILE
LEGAL LIFE
LEGAL MEN

CELL NET AREA
CELL REPLICA
CERE BELLUM
CHAMBERMAIDEN
CHAMBERMAIDS
CHANCERYS
CHANGE CASH CODE
CHANGE INTO
CHANGING NAME
CHANNEL TEN
CHANSER IS
CHAR WOMAN
CHARACTERS
CHARTS CODE
CHATTEL CODE
CHEMICAL FISH
CHEMICAL TAIL
CHEMICAL WAR
CHEST BOX
CHEST KEY
CHICKEN ARSE
CHICKEN MARK
CHILD VOW
CHILD WORD
CHILDS HOME
CHILDS KEY
CHILDS MOM
CHILDS PET
CHIMNEYS
CHIP OF TEN
CHRIST ADAM
CHRIST EGG
CHRIST IDEA
CHRONIC LIE
CHUNNELS
CIRCLES CODE
CIRCLES RACE
CLASS WAR
CLIENT NAME
CLIMBING RACE
CLUCKS HEN
CLUE LESS
COAL FIRE GAS
COBWEBS BASE
CODE FIXING
CODE FOR BIBLE
CODE FOR PEACE
CODE MAPPER
CODE MIXER
CODE OF BLOOD
CODE OF CRIME
CODE OF SEX
CODED ALPHABET
CODED ORIFICE
COILED CYCLE
COILED SEX

LABOUR BASE
LABOUR CODE
LABOUR HAND
LACK OF BLOOD
LACK OF CRIME
LACK OF SEX
LAND BONDING
LAND CENTER
LAND ORIFICE
LAND TOKEN
LATE LUNCH
LATE NIGHT
LATENT ACT
LATEST IDEA
LAUGHABLE GAS
LAUGHABLE RACE
LAW BREAKER
LAW LIST
LAW OF ANGLE
LAW OF TEN
LAW ORDER
LAW POLICE
LAW TRIAL
LAW TRIAL
LAW VOW
LAW WORD
LAW ZONE
LAWS KEY
LAWS LOCK
LAZY COCK
LAZY LIFE
LEARN A PATH
LEARN THEM
LEE OSWALD
LEFT WING
LEGACY MARK
LEGEND OF MAN
LETHAL BALANCE
LETHARGICAL
LETHARGY
LEVEL MIND
LEVERAGE BAR
LEVERAGE BAR
LEXICAL BIBLE
LIARS BEGIN
LIARS HELL
LIARS MODE
LIBARA TOR
LIBERALLY
LIE ENFORCED
LIE ENOUGH
LIE STOP
LIFE ASPECT
LIFE CAGE CYCLE
LIFE CAGE SEX
LIFE DUST

STATE OF BABE
STATED A LIE
STATED CODE
STEEL IMAGE
STEP CHILD
STIFF BONE
STIGMA HAND
STING HAND
STOCK CALL
STOCK MAN
STOMACH ACID
STORES
STUD COCK
STUMBLED
SUCKLE AREA
SUCKLING
SUFFOCATE
SUN DECKS
SUNS END
SWAN DRAKE
SWEARING
TAXREBATE
TEENAGE ANGLE
TEENAGE MATE
TEENAGE TEN
TEENAGE VICE
THE DUNES
THE HIDDEN ADAM
THE HIDDEN DNA
THE HIDDEN IDEA
THE HIDDENEGG
THE RECORD
THE SIGHT
THESE TEN
TO LEAP RACE
TOKEN CASH
TOKEN LAND
TOO FAST
TOYOTA
TUG OF RACE
UMBILIC CODE
UNDER BIDS
VIEWED MAN
WOLVES

LIFE BEGIN	COILED TUBE	LIFE LEVY
LIFE FEED BACK	COINCIDENT	LIFE MA TING
LIFE LIKE	COMBINED CASH	LIFE REPLICA
LIFE SEAL	COMBINED LAND	LIFE TENET
LIFE TAKE	COME INSIDE	LIFES PATH
LIFE UP	COMES AND GO	LIFO JOB CODE
LIFES HEAD	COMING TO	LIGHT A CANDLE
LIGHT AGE	COMMON END	LIGHT BEACON
LIGHT ID	COMPELLABLE	LIGHT MIND
LIMBO HEAD	COMPETES	LIMBO BRIDGE
LIONS	CONCEAL MARK	LINE DEFICIT
LIS TED	CONCLUDES	LINOLEIC ACID
LOAD UP	CONDUCIVE	LION BODY
LOINS	CONJUGATE	LIONS BASE
LOSER	CONJURE A ACE	LIPS HOLE
LOWS	CONTEST	LIVE CRAFT
MAFIA HOLD	COOL KID BASE	LIVE CYCLE
MAFIA MATE	COPS BLOCK	LIVE HEADING
MAFIA MEAT	COPTIC BIBLE	LIVE LONG
MAFIA TEAM	COPY SIDE	LIVE SEX
MAGNUM	CORNER END	LIVES ON
MANDE LAS	COSMO GAIN	LOG ON NAME
MANDELAS	COSMO LAND	LOGO MONAD
MANYANA	COSTUME	LOGO OF GOD
MAPPER	COUNCILS	LONG LIVE
MASSAGED	COUNTER	LOOK LEFT
MATH BASE	COURTS	LOVE FISH
MATH CODE	COWARDS AGE	LOVE WAR
MATIZ	COWARDS ID	LOW FATS
MAY DAY	CRACK THE CODE	LOW RACES
MAYDAY	CRASHING BACK	LOWER DECK
MEAT MOB	CRAZY END	LOWER END
MEAT PIE	CREDIT UP	LUMINOL
MECHANICAL	CREMATED RACE	LUNACY CAP
MELTS	CRIME CYCLE	LUNAR ARCH
MESSAGE	CRIME FILLED	LUNAR BABY
METCASH	CRIME OF CAIN	LUNAR DAY
MEXICAN	CROSS DEAL	LUNAR MAP
MEXICO	CROSS LEAD	LUNATED IDEA
MID WIFE	CURATOR	LUNCH DEATH
MIDWIFE	CURRI RED	LUNCH DIET
MIND CALM	CURSED GOD	LUNGS END
MIND CUE	CURVE BASE	MACHINERY
MIND PAGE	CYBER KIDS	MADIBAS OMEN
MIND REF	CYBER MARK	MADIBAS TIME
MIND SEE	CYCLAMENABLE	MADNESSEDGE
MINOR	CYCLE OF RED	MAFIA FAMILY
MISSED	CYCLIC KEY	MAFIA FORCES
MIXER	CYCLICAL AIR	MAFIA TYPE
MODEL T	CYCLICISM	MAFIAS DOOM
MODEMS	CYCLOID AREA	MAFIAS LEGEND
MODERN	CYCLONES	MAFIAS MONAD
MODIMO	DAGGA DIET BALANCE	MAFIAS TIME
MOM AND DAD	DAGGA MIND CHIP	MAGIC BRAINS
MOMS DAD	DAGGA RAY LIFE	MAGNETIC ACT
MONZA	DAGNE ALPHABET	MAGNETIC BLADE

MR AFRICA
MUD LAND
MUHHAMAD
NAKED FREE
NAME FIELD
NET WEB
NEW BALL
NEW BASE
NEW CODE
NEW HAND
NEW RACE
NILE LAKE
NO BLUE
NO BUDDHA
NO DOPE
NO E MAIL
NO FOOD
NO HIER
NO HOLE
NO LINE
NO MIND
NO PAIN
NO SCALE
NO TABLE
NOTABLE
NOTAS
NOUS
OLD IDEAS
ON A DOT
ON DOPE
ON E MAIL
ON FILM
ON FILM
ON LINE
ON MIND
ON SCALE
ON US
ONE BILL
ONE EYE
ONE GAOL
ONE GOAL
ONE IMAGE
ONE MEDAL
ONE NIL
ONUS
OPEN DNA
OPEN IDEA
OPENS
ORDERED
OT NT
OUMAS
OUT AGE
OVAL EGG
PAID FOR
PALM HAND
PAPPAS

DAGNE CENTRE
DAGNE TOKEN
DAM CAPACITY
DANGER FORCE
DANGER MONAD
DANGER TIME
DANGERS CALL
DATE AND TIME
DATE DUAL MAN
DATE QUEER
DATE WOMAN
DAY NOTICE
DEAD CONFLICT
DEAD FACTORS
DEAD MEDICAL EYE
DEAD MEDICAL IMAGE
DEAD PRIMATE
DEAD RECORDS
DEAD WAR LINE
DEADLY BRIDGE
DEADLY LIES
DEADLY PATH
DEAL TALKING
DEALTH HANDS
DEATH DRIVE
DEATH FALL BASE
DEATH LAND CODE
DEATH SCANDLE
DEATH SCIENCE
DEATH STAR
DEATHS ANGEL
DEATHS TEAM
DEEP ABYSS
DELAY ATOM
DELAY DANGER
DEMONIC AIDS
DEMONIC GAY
DEMONIC NAME
DENIZENS
DENSE ATOM
DEODORANT
DESIREDLIFE
DESTINY
DEVILS PI
DEVILS SEA
DIAMETER EDGE
DIETY NAME
DIGITABLE CODE
DIGITABLE DANCE
DIRECT MODE
DIRECTLY
DISAGREE CALL
DISCOS BASE
DISECT BONE
DISECTED CODE
DISH OUT

MAGNETIC GAP
MAKES BABY ACHE
MAKES HIM ACHE
MALE ORIFICE
MAN ESCAPES
MAN OF DOOM
MAN OF TIME
MANDELAS A LIE
MANDELAS RACE
MANDELASCODE
MANIFESTED
MANS DANGER
MARITAL DEAL
MARK ABLE NAME
MARK OF CELL
MARK OF LIFE
MARKET CALL
MARKET MAN
MASKED WIFE
MASKING DEAL
MATES DEATH
MAYBE SACRED
MEAT DIETS
MECHANICAL HAND
MEDI CENTRE
MEDICAL ALIVE
MEDICAL DANGER
MEDICAL EYE AID
MEDICAL LORD
MEDICAL PILL
MEDUSA NAME
MELODY LEAD
MEMBERS OF
MERIDIAN END
MERMAID NAME
MESS MIND
MESSIAH DEAL
METAPHOR
MIDDLE WAY
MIDI TVS
MIDIS TV
MINCES NAME
MIND BEGINS
MIND DEFICIT
MIND DOWN
MIND FEVER
MIND HEALING
MIND INDEX
MIND LIGHT
MIND PAST
MIND WILL
MINDS BLUB
MINDS MODE
MINDSHOCK
MISSED BY
MISSED HAND

PARKER	DIVIDED ANGLE	MIXER CODE
PAST AGE	DIVIDED MEAT	MK ULTRA
PAST ID	DIVIDED NET	MOB FAMILY
PAVATI	DIVIDED TEAM	MOB FORCES
PAVING	DIVIDED TEN	MOB TITLE
PAY BASE	DIVINE NAME	MOB TYPE
PAY CODE	DIVINE SEED	MODERN CODE
PAY HAND	DNA RESEARCH	MODIFIED CASH
PAY JOB	DNA SCIENCES	MODIFIED DAGNE
PEACE FUL	DOCTOR OF	MODIFIED ECHO
PEDIGREE	DODO SCIENCE	MODIFIED HER
PENALLI	DOING TIME	MODIFIED LAND
PEOPLE	DOMINO GAME	MOLDED BLOCK
PESTED	DONT FLY	MOM AND CHILD
PICK AXE	DOOMS ARK	MOMLESS
PICKING	DOOMS DAY	MOMS BONE
PIECE MEAL	DOOMS PIE	MOMS CHILD
PIRATE	DOUAY BIBLE	MOMS LAW
PIRATE	DOUBLE SEAL	MONEY ACT
PORT	DOUBLE SIDE	MONKEY AGE
PRE DATE	DOUBLE UP	MONO GRAM
PRE BIBLE	DRACONIAN BACK	MOON TEAM
PRE PAID	DRANK BLOOD	MOSLEMS
PRIMAL	DREAMLESS	MOTHER BACK
PRO DAGGA	DRUNK MAN	MOTHER ICE
QIGONG	DUAL BLEND OF	MOULDED LEAD
QUEUE	DUAL STAR	MOUTHS
RACE CART	DUST LIFE	MUD LAND RED
RACE WAR	DYNAMIC RACE	MUHAMMAD ALI
RADAR BASE	E TV LOGO	MUHAMMADIM
RADAR CODE	EACH TO MASK	MUSIC ECHO
RADAR HAND	EARLIER MAN	MUSIC LAND
RAIN DANCE	EARTH RAY	MY FATHER
RANG ON	EARTH SPACE	NAKED NEWS
RARE HALF	EARTHS AREA	NAME ADHERENCE
RARE RACE	EARTHS PI	NAME AND OFFICE
RARE RED	EARTHS SEA	NAME CHANGING
RATING	ECHO CENTRE	NAME FACTOR
RC CYCLE	ECONOMICS	NAME OF FIRED
RC THIEF	ECZEMA MARK	NAME OF FISH
RE EVEN	EDGE DISTANCE	NAME OF NEW
REALISE	EDIT SCIENCE	NAME OF SELF
RECESS	EEN SKOOL	NAME OF SIN
RED BITCH	ELAN VITAL	NAME OF WAR
RED CENT	ELASTIC CODE	NAME SEEKER
RED DAWN	ELBOW ANGLE	NASA NEWS
RED FISH	ELECTION AGE	NAZI BODY
RED HOOD	ELECTION ID	NAZI BRANCH
RED LADY	ELECTRIC BEAM	NAZI CRY
RED TAPE	ELECTRIC FAN	NAZI DRAIN
REDEEMS	ELECTRIFIED	NAZI HANDS
REEL ON	ELEPHANT FACE	NAZI HERO
REF MIND	ELUDE DANGER	NAZI PAPAL
REGOES	ELUDED PATH	NAZIS BASE
RELAXED	ELUDEDGODS	NAZIS CODE
RELEASED	EMBARRASS	NAZIS HAND

REMAINED	EMBODY LIFE	NEO LUMP
REWARD	EMPLOYEE	NEO PLASMA
RICKSHA	EMULATES	NEO QUEEN
RILEY	ENCYCLIC DOC	NERVE BOMB
ROAD LAND	ENCYCLICAL DAD	NERVE CELL
ROAD RAGE	END OF EARTH	NERVE LIFE
ROB ONE	END OF FORM	NET AND GRID
ROE LAND	END OF STAGE	NEW CHEMICAL
ROLES	END OFFERER	NEW DIALECT
ROMANCE	ENDEMIAL SEED	NEW EYES
ROME HEAD	ENDEMIC MARK	NEW GAME CALL
ROOI DAG	ENDEMICAL BABY	NEW IMAGES
RYOBI	ENDEMICAL BUG	NEW LOVE
SACRED ADAM	ENDEMICAL MAP	NEW SUN
SACRED DNA	ENDLESS HEAD	NEWS EYE
SACRED IDEA	ENERGY DEAL	NEWS IMAGE
SACRED RA	ENGINEERS	NO BASE LINE
SACREDEGG	ENIGMATIC FACE	NO CHALLENGE
SALLY	ENTIRE AREA	NO ESTEEM
SAMCOR	ENUNCIATED	NO EVIDENCE
SAME LAND	EPISCOPAL	NO FAIRIES
SAP NAME	ETHERIC CALL	NO NOBLES
SARAFINA	EUGENE TEAM	NO POLIO
SAT ON	EURO RAND	NO SONS
SAUCY	EVIL BLOOD	NO SOUL
SAW GOD	EVIL CRAFT	NO WATER
SCORN	EVIL HEADING	NORWAY
SEE E MAIL	EVIL SEX	NOSE EARS
SEE FOOD	EXACT CATS	NOT TRACE
SEEN GOD	EXISTS	NP JUDGES
SELF EGO	EXPAND CELL	NUCLEI CELL
SHAM BALLA	EXPAND LIFE	NUMBER END
SHAME END	EYE TO GOD	NUMBER I AM
SHAVEN	FACE OF POLICE	NUMERICAL
SINGABLE	FACE PROFILE	NURSE AIDE
SLACKER	FACE THE EVIL	NURSES
SLICE OF	FACULTIES	OBSTACLES
SLOW	FAIR RIGHT	ODD BI QUEEN
SLOW	FAIR STANCE	ODD NUMBER
SMASHED	FAIR TAKING	OF A CROSS
SMELT	FALSE RUN	OF A MESSIAH
SMITH	FAMILY BABY	OF DIAMETER
SNACK BAR	FAMILY BIBLE	OF DISTANCE
SNAKE EGG	FAMILY DAY	OFF THE CUFF
SNAKES	FAMILY MAFIA	OFF THE FIELD
SNAPS	FAMILY MAP	OFFERED HELL
SON OF	FAMILY MOB	OFFERED RAND
SOOT	FARM SCIENCE	OFFERED UP
SPITE	FASTER HAND	OFFERER END
SREVE	FASTER RACE	OFFERERD IDEA
STARCH	FATHER AFRICA	OLD CENTRE
STARK	FATTENING	OLD TIMER
STATED	FAVORITE	OMENS BABY
STELLA	FIDUCIARY	ON KEEPING
STENCH	FIELD OF ANGLE	ON WEAK RACE
STEP DAD	FIELD OF TEN	ONE ACTION

STEPED	FIELD OF VICE	ONE BALLOT
STING	FINAL RACE CODE	ONE CARDINAL
SUFFICE	FIRE SCIENCE	ONE CONCEALED
SUIT	FIRM GRIP	ONE GOD CHILD
SUMP	FIRST ACT	ONE GOD LAW
SUN FACE	FIRST AID BAG	ONE HOUR
TAXES	FIRST CAT	ONE MARGIN
THE LAW	FIRST ERA	ONE PAPACY
THE LAW	FIRST KID	ONE QUEEN
THE TAO	FIRST X	ONE SHOT
TO LEAP	FISH BODIES	ONE UNDER
WEALTH	FISH LOVE	ONE VOTE

Conclusion

Letter to my students

MANY SO-CALLED EXPERTS WILL COME TO THE CONCLUSION THAT YOU HAVE JUST FINISHED
READING A TEXT THAT IS BASED ON 'NOTHING MORE' THAN A PLAY OF WORDS. TO DRAW ANY OTHER
CONCLUSION WOULD BE DETRIMENTAL TO THEIR OWN LEARNINGS. IT WOULD MEAN THAT
"EVERYTHING" THAT THEY HAVE LEARNT IN LIFE...ABOUT LIFE, WAS TOTALLY WRONG. TO ADMIT TO
SUCH "ERROR" IS NOT WITHIN THE DESIGN OF EITHER SCIENCE OR RELIGION. HOWEVER, THE
KNOWLEDGE "I" IMPART TO YOU WAS NOT DESIGNED FOR THEIR UNDERSTANDING. SCIENCE AND
RELIGION ARE BOTH INCAPABLE OF UNDERSTANDING THE 'SIMPLICITIES-OF-LIFE'. THE ONLY WAY
TO OVERCOME THEIR PERVERTED CONTROL OVER OUR PERSONAL LIVES IS TO COME-UP WITH A
PURE THEORY THAT COVERS THE FULL SPECTRUM OF LIFE...INCLUDING THEIR OWN RESPECTIVE
TEACHINGS.

WHAT SCIENCE CALLS "ENERGY"...OUR CHURCH FATHERS' CALL "JESUS/GOD SON".
WHAT SCIENCE CALLS "MATTER"...OUR CHURCH-FATHERS' CALL "CHRIST/THE GOD-HEAD".
FOR NEITHER THE FORMER OR LATTER CAN BE "CREATED OR DESTROYED"...BY MAN.
SINCE TIME IMMEMORIAL, BOTH SCIENCE AND RELIGION HAVE HAD A FIELDSDAY IN SILENCING
THE MESSENGER...BUT HAVE NEVER BEEN SUCCESSFUL IN DESTROYING THE *"MESSAGE"*{*69}.

MESSAGE (*69)...LIVES ON(*96):

"THE DANCE OF THE MATRIX" IS BASED ON A COLLECTION OF "HEADINGS AND sub-HEADINGS" I HAVE COLLECTED
OVER THE PAST NINETEEN YEARS OF RESEARCH. I BECAME A GRAND-MASTER OUT OF THE NATURAL DESIGN OF
CREATION. I CAN OFFER NO EXCUSE IN DEFENCE OF MY WORK...EXCEPT, I SUPPOSE, IS THE FOLLOWING
FACTORS:

a] I DID NOT INVENT THE "ROMAN/LATIN ALPHABET" FROM 'A to Z', NOR DID I INSTRUCT SCIENCE
OR RELIGION TO LAY OUT THE ROMAN ALPHABET IN SUCH A "NUMERICAL(*96)" WAY...THAT 'A'
WOULD BE FIRST, 'B' WOULD BE SECOND, 'C' WOULD BE THIRD...AND 'Z' TO BE LAST.
b] I DID NOT INVENT THE ROMAN NUMERALS NOR THE ARABIC NUMERALS.
c] I DID NOT WRITE THE BIBLE...NOR ANY BOOK THAT CLAIMS TO BE A MESSAGE FROM GOD.
d] I DID NOT NAME THE SONS OF GOD...TO BE JESUS, MESSIAH, THE OMEGA, LUCIFER, AND SO ON.
e] I DID NOT INSINUATE THAT THE NUMBER OF THE BEAST WAS *666 OR *616.
f] I DID NOT INSINUATE...QUOTE. "This calls for Wisdom, let him who has understanding calculate the
Number of the BEAST; for it is a Human Number." Ref: REVELATION 13:18
g] I DID NOT CHOOSE MY NAME... NOR THE DATE OF MY BIRTH.
h] I DID NOT CHOOSE MY PARENTS' GENETIC CODE.

I] MOST OF ALL...I DID NOT FOLLOW MY FATHER'S FOOTSTEP AND CONTINUE TO REPEAT HIS MISTAKES. I FOLLOWED MY OWN MISTAKES AND COUNTED MY CROSSES FOR EACH MISTAKE I WAS FORCED TO CORRECT. I AM MY OWN MAN AND MASTER...FOR I HAVE NO TEACHER.

*THE GRAND MASTER OF GONTIERISM:
DARRELL JOSEPH ROGER GONTIER

I am now going to tELL YOU A STORY, AND AT THE CONCLUSION OF EACH STORY I TELL, I SHALL CALCULATE THE VALUE OF WHAT I HAVE STATED.

IT WILL BE LEFT TO YOU TO CALCULATE THE VERACITY OF MY STATEMENT.

AS ALL THINGS CAN BE RELATED IN TERMS OF " **69** " And " **96** ", in order to demonstrate the true meaning of "L-- I F --E ". in terms of **THE LOGO** IF WHICH RESIDES IN THE CENTER OF "L-- I F --E ".

IN TERMS OF **THE LOGO**, THE TWO SYMBOLS WHICH RESIDES IN THE WORD "**L--** I F **--E** " PLAYS AN IMPORTANT ROLE IN DEMONSTRATING IT'S RELATIONSHIP, IN TERMS OF TRUTH.

THE LETTER " **I** " IS THE **9**TH LETTER IN THE ROMAN ALPHABET, AND THE LETTER " **F** " IS THE **6**TH LETTER. WHEN "L-- I F --E " IS SEPERATED, BY EVIL MEN, IN THEIR WHITE NIGHTIES, THE NUMBER " **9** " AND THE NUMBER " **6** " SPIN AROUND, AND REVEAL THEMSELVES AS " **69** "! SO, ALTHOUGH "**THE CHIP**" WAS **"CONDUCIVE"** TO "THE WHOLE", THEY

*G-TRAIN... ON-LINE... FOR MAFIA... MUST END... TODAY- A - DAY...
NO NOBLES... ON-BOARD... FREE TRAIN... TO FREE... Mr. AFRICA... FATHER AFRICA...
SAME FATHER... SAME SCIENCE... SAME STAR... PICTURED... ON-FILM...
WAS LIE... CONDUCIVE... TO ONE RACE.

<u>NOTAS</u>:

PEOPLE... PICTURED... ON-FILM... TO YOU... FROM SPACE... BY A ALIEN RACE...
ON-BOARD... SPACE-SHIP... WAS A AFRICAN... CALLED "L-- I F --E ".

HIS NAME (CODE)... WAS GOD... A JEHOVAH GOD... IN PARADISE... WITH FEET...

HARMONIC RELATIONSHIPS BETWEEN ALL WORDS AND NUMBERS:

The Matrix

20
9 **10** 11
0
     1

21
10 **11** 12
1
     11

22
11 **12** 13
2
     21

23
12 **13** 14
3
     31

24
13 **14** 15
4
     41

25
14 **15** 16
5
     51

26
15 **16** 17
6
     61

27
16 **17** 18
7
     71

28
17 **18** 19
8
     81

29
18 **19** 20
9
     91

30
19 **20** 21
10
     2

31
20 **21** 22
11
     12

32
21 **22** 23
12

                22

        33
    22 **23** 24
        13
                32

        34
    23 **24** 25
        14
                42

        35
    24 **25** 26
        15
                52

        36
    25 **26** 27
        16
                62

        37
    26 **27** 28
        17
                72

        38
    27 **28** 29
        18
                82

        39
    28 **29** 30
        19
                92

        40
    29 **30** 31
        20
                03

        41
    30 **31** 32
        21
                13

        42
    31 **32** 33
        22
                23

        43
    32 **33** 34
        23
                33

        44
    33 **34** 35
        24
                43

        45
    34 **35** 36
        25
                53

        46

35 **36** 37
  26
      63

  47
36 **37** 38
  27
      73

  48
37 **38** 39
  28
      83

  49
38 **39** 40
  29
      93

  50
39 **40** 41
  30
      04

  51
40 **41** 42
  31
      14

  52
41 **42** 43
  32
      24

  53
42 **43** 44
  33
      34

  54
43 **44** 45
  34
      44

  55
44 **45** 46
  35
      54

  56
45 **46** 47
  36
      64

  57
46 **47** 48
  37
      74

  58
47 **48** 49
  38
      84

  59
48 **49** 50
  39
      94

        60
49 **50** 51
        40
                5

        61
50 **51** 52
        41
                15

        62
51 **52** 53
        42
                25

        63
52 **53** 54
        43
                35

        64
53 **54** 55
        44
                45

        65
54 **55** 56
        45
                55

        66
55 **56** 57
        46
                65

        67
56 **57** 58
        47
                75

        68
57 **58** 59
        48
                85

        69
58 **59** 60
        49
                95

        70
59 **60** 61
        50
                6

        71
60 **61** 62
        51
                16

        72
61 **62** 63
        52
                26

        73

62 **63** 64
53
    36

74
63 **64** 65
54
    46

75
64 **65** 66
55
    56

76
65 **66** 67
56
    99

77
66 **67** 68
57
    76

78
67 **68** 69
58
    86

79
68 **69** 70
59
    96

80
69 **70** 71
60
    7

81
70 **71** 72
61
    17

82
71 **72** 73
62
    27

83
72 **73** 74
63
    37

84
73 **74** 75
64
    47

85
74 **75** 76
65
    57

86
75 **76** 77
66
    67

87
76 **77** 78
67
     77

88
77 **78** 79
68
     87

89
78 **79** 80
69
     97

90
79 **80** 81
70
     8

91
80 **81** 82
71
     18

92
81 **82** 83
72
     28

93
82 **83** 84
73
     38

94
83 **84** 85
74
     48

95
84 **85** 86
75
     58

96
85 **86** 87
76
     68

97
86 **87** 88
77
     78

98
87 **88** 89
78
     88

99
88 **89** 90
79
     98

100
89 **90** 91
80
     9

101

```
90 91 92
   81
         19


      102
91 92 93
   82
         29


      103
92 93 94
   83
         39


      104
93 94 95
   84
         49


      105
94 95 96
   85
         59


      106
95 96 97
   86
         69


      107
96 97 98
   87
         79


      108
97 98 99
   88
         89


      109
98 99 100
   89
         66


...
```

The Modern Dance of the Ying and Yang

www.ingramcontent.com/pod-product-compliance
Lightning Source LLC
Chambersburg PA
CBHW051345290326
41933CB00042B/3240